Chef on the Run

Run

Simply the Best

DIANE CLEMENT

Chef on the Run

Simply the Best

Favourite Recipes from the Bestselling Series,

Plus Exciting New Dishes

RAINCOAST BOOKS

Vancouver

Raincoast Books acknowledges the ongoing financial support of the Government of
Canada through the Canada Council for the Arts and the Book Publishing Industry
Development Program (BPIDP); and the Government of British Columbia through the
BC Arts Council.

Design by Ingrid Paulson
Photography by John Sherlock

NATIONAL LIBRARY OF CANADA CATALOGUING IN PUBLICATION DATA
Clement, Diane, 1936–
    Best of chef on the run

    Includes index.
    ISBN 1-55192-563-X

    1. Cookery. 2. Entertaining. 3. Menus. I. Title.

TX731.C588 2002   641.5   C2002-910564-1

LIBRARY OF CONGRESS CATALOGUE NUMBER: 2002091850

Raincoast Books   In the United States:
9050 Shaughnessy Street   Publishers Group West
Vancouver, British Columbia   1700 Fourth Street
Canada   V6P 6E5   Berkeley, California
www.raincoast.com   94710

At Raincoast Books we are committed to protecting the environment and to the
responsible use of natural resources. We are acting on this commitment by working
with suppliers and printers to phase out our use of paper produced from ancient
forests. This book is one step towards that goal. It is printed on 100% ancient-forest-
free paper (100% post-consumer recycled), processed chlorine- and acid-free, and
supplied by Rolland. It is printed with vegetable-based inks. For further information,
visit our website at www.raincoast.com. We are working with Markets Initiative
(www.oldgrowthfree.com) on this project.

Printed in Canada by Transcontinental Printing

10 9 8 7 6 5 4 3 2 1

TABLE OF CONTENTS

INTRODUCTION

I t's hard to believe it was 20 years ago that my cooking class students encouraged me to write my first cookbook, *Chef on the Run*. They would say, "I use the recipes from your classes so often that I can't read them anymore — why don't you put them in a book?" Even 20 years later I meet people who say, "Diane, my *Chef on the Run* is worn out, I use it so often." *More Chef on the Run*, *Chef and Doctor on the Run* and *Fresh Chef on the Run* have been equally popular and Canadian bestsellers.

So when my longtime publisher, Raincoast Books, asked, "Diane, how do you feel about doing an anniversary book including the most irresistible recipes from the Chef series as well your newest favourites?" I replied, "When do we start?"

~

The hot food trends in the new millennium, as they did 20 years ago, definitely favour "comfort foods." Whether preparing meals for a busy family on the run or for special entertaining, we are searching for quick-to-prepare recipes that are not intimidating and won't break the bank!

Over the past five decades my husband Doug and I have had the privilege of travelling the world with the Canadian Olympic team and for our sports medicine seminars, Lifestyle lectures and family vacations. One of the joys of international travel was the opportunity to eat our way around the world, and later recreating the dishes in my own kitchen. Chefs and friends have also shared their special recipes with me. To my selections for this book I have added the "star dishes" that have shone in my cooking classes, restaurant, and best of all, from feeding my family and entertaining friends.

The thrill for me is sharing these culinary journeys with you. The recipes are simplified for our busy schedules, and I've included menu ideas for your special dinner parties.

As well, "Diane's Secrets" will help make your time in the kitchen pleasurable. Remember, cooking can be fun!

As your "chef on the run," I will start you off on the right track: Are you ready? On your marks … set … cook!

KITCHEN ESSENTIALS

Every chef, professional or amateur, has his or her "must have" kitchen tools and specific equipment he or she can't do without. Just as athletes insist on wearing their lucky pieces of equipment or clothing whenever they compete, chefs likewise rely on their favourite kitchen utensils to help ensure the success of their recipes. Whenever I teach a cooking class, the participants ask, "What are your favourite kitchen utensils?" I could go on for pages on what a complete dream kitchen would have, but along with the basic utensils and equipment, the items that follow are the essentials of my kitchen.

The first word of advice is to invest in the best you can afford in whatever kitchen equipment you purchase, big or small. In the long run, the better-quality brands will outlast and outperform the cheaper bands. For major investments, do your research ahead of time and seek the advice of kitchen specialists before making a purchase.

The second word of advice is to take time to browse through kitchen specialty shops at home or on your travels. Often you will come across the latest "hot" piece of kitchen equipment for making your cooking chores simpler.

MY FAVOURITE EQUIPMENT
LARGER ITEMS

- **Food processor**: Couldn't do without it! Keep it on your counter, not in a back cupboard.
- **Electronic mixer or hand mixer**: Many brands offer multi-use additional pieces.
- **Blender**: A must for fruit drinks, some sauces.
- **Mandolin**: Wonderful for slicing vegetables for gratins, salads and so on. The Japanese plastic ones work well, if you don't want to invest in the more expensive European variety.
- **Espresso machine**: Must admit, we've had ours for over two years and we still don't use it! One of these days, I'll get the urge.

KNIVES

Can't stress enough, invest in the best! After opening our restaurant I was totally intimidated over using the larger chef's knives and much preferred the middle-size chopping knives.

The key knives in my collection:
- German: Henckels 4-inch slicing knife
- German: Henckels 6-inch slicing knife
- German: Henckels bread knife
- Japanese: Global G-5 7-inch chopping knife
- Japanese: Global Millennium 5-inch slicing knife
- Swiss: Victorinox 4-inch inexpensive tomato-slicer knife

POTS AND PANS

I would never recommend purchasing "a set" of pots and pans! I would rather choose multi-use ones that I use often, such as large sauté pan or large fry pan. My choices:
- Assorted Teflon pans for omelettes and the like
- Calphalon: large sauté pans with straight sides for sauces, etc.
- Calphalon: large fry pan
- Assorted stainless steel pots
- Roaster pan
- Dutch oven
- Stock pot (if you have time to make stock!)
- Wok is recommended, but I must admit I don't have one.
- Specialty baking pans, for example flan pans, springform pans
- Assorted gratin dishes and lasagna-type ceramic casseroles that can go to the table

THE LITTLE HELPERS

- Pepper mill (Peugeot is the best. I have the large and the latest mini silver one for travelling!)
- Zester: for citrus fruits
- Reamer: wooden for juicing is the best
- Assorted wooden spoons, spatulas and whisks
- Garlic press
- Strainers of varied meshes and sizes
- Parchment paper for baking sheets
- Pastry bag, etc., for the avid baker and artist
- A corkscrew that works! Check with your specialty stores and wine stores

MENU PLANNING

Food is enjoyed most when it's shared. It doesn't require a special birthday or anniversary to give us the incentive to invite family and friends over to enjoy good food and lively conversation, and a meal doesn't have to blow your month's budget, either!

WHAT WILL I SERVE?

The biggest challenge is establishing the menu. The occasion could be as simple as a late-morning brunch, a hearty après-ski dinner, a summer barbecue on the patio, or a spontaneous get-together. Whatever it may be, these tips and menus will make life easier when entertaining.

CHEF ON THE RUN?

Many dishes in this book can be prepared ahead of time to eliminate last-minute stress. Don't invite too many guests: I feel the ideal number is six to eight; you get time to enjoy all the conversation and it's more manageable serving the courses.

KITCHEN DRAMA

Entertaining is a stage production of sorts. You are the producer/director creating the drama! I always feel that curtain-up adrenalin rush no matter how many times I've entertained over the decades. Once the guests arrive, we start an evening of food, fun and entertainment.

ARE YOU MISSING OUT ON YOUR OWN PARTY?

Often the host or hostess spends most of the time in the kitchen, rushing around to complete dishes at the last minute. Plan your menu around your time schedule, budget and size of your home or condo. Remember, it has to be fun for you, too! We are entertaining much less formally than we ever have, with our guests willing to pitch in to toss a salad or turn the salmon on the barbecue.

DON'T GO CRAZY IF TIME RUNS OUT

If you don't have time to prepare all the suggested menu dishes, substitute with your favourite gourmet take-out and bakery specialties. As one of my cooking experts bluntly puts it, "Buy and lie!"

SPECIAL REQUESTS

With so many food allergies and special diets today, we also have to address this issue when inviting guests. There's nothing more disappointing than doing a fantastic salmon barbecue only to find that half of the guests are allergic to salmon. You can always add chicken or other seafood if you know in advance.

I CAN'T BELIEVE IT!

You can't always win. When I nervously held one of my first dinner parties, I decided to do a succulent butterflied leg of lamb on the barbecue. As I was turning it over on the grill, I heard one of the guests exclaim to another, "I hate lamb!" So I rushed to the freezer, quickly thawed a chicken breast and barbecued it to a good "charcoal" black (by mistake, of course!). Before I served it I poured myself a good glass of wine and joined the guests. From that time on I have always asked my guests when I invite them, "Is there anything you *don't* like?"

OH MY GOD! IT'S A DINNER PARTY!

We've all faced the embarrassment of misjudging the occasion. When inviting guests, always be specific that it's a dinner party so they won't arrive an hour or more late, thinking it's a casual drop-in for cocktails and appetizers. Embarrassing for everyone, especially if you feel obligated to eat a "second" dinner!

MENUS

Here are 10 menu ideas using various recipes found in this book — something for every occasion.

COME FOR BRUNCH!

There is something totally relaxing about a long leisurely weekend brunch. Invite your friends over around 11 a.m. and expect them to leave around 3 p.m.! No one will be in a rush.

Keep it simple. Starting off with preparing the Frittata Primavera a day ahead. Give your guests the option of adding sparkling wine to their orange juice; it doesn't have to be expensive champagne or sparkling wine. Pick up the baked goods from your favourite bakery and serve them warm.

> **Freshly squeezed orange juice with champagne, or add to the orange juice a good shot of French Liquor Alize (a blend of passion fruit juice and cognac)**
>
> **Frittata Primavera (pg. 143) OR Linda's Caramel Apple French Toast (pg. 138)**
>
> **Bread basket: assorted scones, bagels, croissants**
>
> **Homemade jams, jellies, cream cheese or mascarpone cheese**
>
> **Fresh fruit platter with French vanilla yogurt**
>
> **Bottomless pot of coffee**

APRÈS-SKI

After a long day on the slopes snowboarding, cross-country or downhill skiing, your body craves "comfort foods." Red wine and chilled beer would go well with the classic French Canadian Tourtière with Sour Cream Sauce. Get a jump-start on the menu by doing the salad dressing, tourtière and lemon cake ahead of time. The tourtière can be made a day or two ahead and refrigerated, or frozen weeks before serving. The lemon cake also freezes well. If frozen, thaw in the refrigerator overnight.

Mediterranean Baked Chèvre Olive Appetizer (pg. 22)

Spinach-Grapefruit Salad (pg. 91)

French Canadian Tourtière with Sour Cream Sauce (pg. 196)

Sourdough bread

Jen and Vincent's Lemon Cake with Seasonal Berries (pg. 206)

VIVA ITALIA

This is an easy do-ahead Italian menu that I rely on for many informal dinner parties. Include some Italian wines to complement the dishes, then finish with a smooth "pick-me-up" ice cream finale.

Olive Cheese Balls (pg. 35)

Roasted Asparagus-Bocconcini Salad (pg. 82)

Tuscan Chicken with Orzo (pg. 176) or Lamb Shanks with Orzo (pg. 190)

Ice Cream with Espresso and Frangelico (pg. 214)

Italian biscotti or macaroons

ROMANTICALLY FRENCH

My choice for an anniversary or birthday celebration, there's something about French cuisine that brings out the romanticism in all of us! It's elegant, but at the same time gutsy. Start off with a surprise bubbly, a Roasted Beet and Chèvre Tart first course, the Provence roasted chicken and potato entrée, ending with a Chocolate Almond Velvet or French Fruit Clafoutis. The beauty of this menu is that it can all be prepared ahead of time. If the cherries aren't in season, go for the Sparkling Shiraz or Rosé Brut on its own.

> Frosted Cherries with Rosé Brut or Sparkling Shiraz (pg. 58)
>
> Rand and Suzie's Roasted Beet and Chèvre Tart (pg. 40)
>
> Basil Roasted Chicken With Garlic Sauce (pg. 177)
>
> Potatoes Gratin (pg. 123)
>
> Stuffed Tomatoes à la Provençal (pg. 128) or Roasted Vegetables (pg. 126)
>
> Chocolate Almond Velvet (pg. 215) or French Fruit Clafoutis (pg. 222)

A TASTE OF ASIA

Beijing, Shanghai and Singapore were the highlights of a trip we made to Asia in 2001. This menu represents the many dishes we enjoyed as we toured these magnificent cities, starting off with the famous Singapore Sling, which originated at Singapore's majestic Hotel Raffles.

> Singapore Sling (pg. 55)
>
> New York Duck Salad with Crispy Wontons (pg. 104)
>
> Pork Tenderloin Superb (pg. 195)
>
> Oriental Fried Vegetable Rice (pg. 114)
>
> Singaporean Spicy Asparagus and Shiitake Mushroom Sauce (pg. 131)
>
> Mango-Lime Champagne Ice (pg. 216)

PICNIC IN THE PARK

Warm, balmy summer days and evenings are a perfect excuse to pack a picnic into your basket and head off to the nearest beach or park. Choose easy foods packed in lots of dry ice to keep everything cold and safe. This menu was created for a Father's Day picnic, so we wanted it to be très chic! If you happen to wake up to a rainstorm, the picnic works beautifully at home!

> Strawberries 'n Champagne Soup (pg. 72)
>
> Chicken Breasts Supreme (pg. 173) with Wild Rice Salad (pg. 94)

Prawn and Cherry Tomato Salad (pg. 90)

Champagne Zabaglione Berry Gratin (pg. 224)

Dianne's Rice Krispies Chocolate Chip Cookies (pg. 201)

TURKISH-MOROCCAN DELIGHTS

Full of intense flavour and colour, the foods of the Middle East and the Balkans are always a big hit at any dinner party. Most of the dishes can be prepared in advance, which I love.

Turkish Meze (pg. 46)

Pita bread, Mediterranean flat bread

Annette's Moroccan Roasted Chicken (pg. 181)

Couscous with Chick Peas (pg. 117)

Liz's Heavenly Lemon Mousse (pg. 221)

Turkish delights, figs, pistachio nuts

Mint tea

HAWAIIAN SUNSETS

During our stay at our friends Gerry and Bill Gartside's condo in Maui, Doug and I enjoyed watching the vibrant sunsets most evenings from their lanai. The abundance of fresh fish, fruits and vegetables made it so easy for me to whip up a Hawaiian dinner that we had no desire to dine out. This menu would be ideal for summertime entertaining anywhere, with pleasant images of the tropical paradise of Hawaii. Substitute the Maui onions, tomatoes and salt with local sweet onions, on-the-vine tomatoes and sea salt.

Rosé Wine with Pineapple (pg. 57)

Macadamia nuts

Chilled Melon Soup (pg. 73)

> **Maui Prawns with Mango-Macadamia Nut Salsa (pg. 31) or**
>   **Seared Tuna Salad (pg. 100)**
> **Sliced Maui onions and beefsteak tomatoes, Maui salt, Balsamic**
>   **Vinaigrette (pg. 107)**
> **Mango Panna Cotta (pg. 228) or fresh pineapple and mangoes**

TEX-MEX-SANTA FE

For informal dining that everyone enjoys, American southwestern cuisine is the answer. I presented this menu on the *Vicki Gabereau Show* on CTV television. Vicki pitched in to assist me in whipping up this menu. As always, Vicki was humorous and witty and we laughed the whole time! This menu is definitely a southwestern teaser. Surprise your guests with a new twist to the traditional guacamole by starting off with Guacamole on the Half Shell or serve a Tequila-Spiked Avocado-Shrimp Cocktail. This will start their taste buds soaring! Follow that with a fun Mexican Torta that allows you to use your imagination and create your own version. The unusual Aztec Ice Cream with Lime Sauce will linger with your guests as they head for home. Take a trip to your local Mexican deli and pick up most of the ingredients; the rest is easy!

> **Mexican beer**
> **Guacamole on the Half Shell (pg. 29)**
>   **or Tequila-Spiked Avocado-Shrimp Cocktail (pg. 30)**
> **Mexican Torta (Chilaquiles) (pg. 186)**
>   **or Cal-Mex Chicken Fiesta (pg. 184)**
> **Condiments: sour cream, tomato salsa, guacamole,**
>   **chopped cilantro, chopped green onions**
> **Corn chips, assorted colours**
> **Aztec Ice Cream with Lime Sauce (pg. 220)**

HALIBUT MANGO TANGO

I love halibut and sea bass, and this menu I serve often when stocks are at their peak. The marriage of these delicate fish and the sweet taste of fresh mango is delightful. Thai Rice with Coconut Milk goes perfectly with this entrée, along with fresh asparagus or snow peas. To tease the palate, I would start off with Vicki's smoked salmon appetizer.

> **Vicki's Smoked Salmon and Potato Crisps with Wasabi Cream (pg. 45)**
>
> **Seasonal greens with Orange Mustard Dressing (pg. 110)**
>
> **Halibut Mango Tango (pg. 164)**
>
> **Thai Rice with Coconut Milk (pg. 115)**
>
> **Asparagus or snow peas**
>
> **Raspberry and White Chocolate Tart (pg. 230)**

Appetiz

ers

MEDITERRANEAN BAKED CHÈVRE OLIVE APPETIZER

Serves 4–6

Santorini in Greece, perched on top of a volcanic site, its quaint buildings painted white and ancient churches identified by their sky blue domes, has to be one of the most magical and romantic islands in the world. The cuisine was equally enticing. This particular dish was quickly devoured by Doug and me as we dined at one of Santorini's popular cliff restaurants. We were surprised and delighted to discover that the island also produces some favourable wines, not just the traditional retsina.

10 oz	soft chèvre cheese	250 g
⅓ cup	kalamata olives, pitted	80 mL
2 tbsp	toasted pine nuts	30 mL
6	pita bread	6

MARINADE:

2 tbsp	olive oil	30 mL
	zest of 1 lemon	
2 tbsp	lemon juice	30 mL
1 tbsp	fresh basil, chopped	15 mL
1 tbsp	fresh oregano, chopped	15 mL
½ tsp	sweet paprika	2.5 mL
	pepper to taste	

METHOD:

Early on the day of serving, mound the chèvre cheese in a 6-in/15-cm baking dish. Drizzle the marinade mixture evenly across the top of the cheese. Sprinkle the olives over all. Refrigerate until ready to bake.

In a small bowl, combine the marinade ingredients and set aside.

Just before serving, bake in 400°F/200°C oven for 10–15 minutes, or until heated through.

Sprinkle with the pine nuts. Serve with warmed pita bread, sliced into small triangles.

SALMON SEDUCTION APPETIZER

Serves 2

The Wickaninnish Inn, situated at Chesterman Beach near Tofino and Pacific Rim National Park Reserve, is truly outstanding. Designated as one of the prestigious "Relais & Chateau" inns of the world, it is headed by general manager Charles McDiarmid, and its Winter Storm Package is famous. All guestrooms and the dining room have views of the wind-whipped surf of the Pacific Ocean. The West Coast decor that showcases the exquisite First Nations art is superb. Every room has a warm fireplace enticing you to relax, read your newest book or just listen to the roaring surf! The inn's Ancient Cedars Spa is ideal after a brisk walk along the beach or after kayaking. The Pointe Restaurant, overlooking the ocean, has won accolades worldwide for its ambience, service and fresh seafood. Award-winning chef de cuisine Jim Garraway loves to tantalize our taste buds with little teasers such as the whimsical presentation of his Salmon Seduction appetizer.

This recipe is my adaptation of that dish. It's best served at the dinner table; just multiply the ingredients for the number of guests you are serving.

3	**thin smoked salmon slices**	3
3 tbsp	**Boursin cheese with garlic and herbs, or chèvre**	45 mL
1	**baguette, thinly sliced**	1

METHOD:

Lay the smoked salmon slices flat on a chopping board. Spread each with 1 tbsp/15 mL of the Boursin cheese or chèvre. Roll up in jelly roll-fashion, starting with the widest end. Refrigerate until ready to serve.

SALMON PRESENTION:

Smoked Salmon Rolls with Boursin, one roll per person; Indian pepper candy salmon, 2 wedges (½ in/1 cm) per person; maple smoked salmon, 2 wedges (½ in/1 cm) per person; salmon jerky, 1 piece (2 in/5 cm) per person, sliced into 3 thin strips each.

DIANE'S SECRETS:

You can experiment with other specialty salmon, such as barbecued, lox — whatever your fish market may feature. You be the artist and create whatever combinations you wish!

TO SERVE:

Slice the Smoked Salmon with Boursin in three diagonal pieces per roll. In the middle of each plate, place 3 Smoked Salmon rolls and the Indian pepper candy salmon. Place a martini glass on top of the salmon presentation. On the base of the martini glass, arrange the Maple Smoked Salmon wedges and the Salmon Jerky. When eating, start with the salmon on the base of the martini glass, then remove the glass and start in on the salmon on the plate. Serve with a basket of sliced baguette.

SHRIMP AND CORN FRITTERS

Makes about 24, serves 4–6 as appetizers

I have been co-hosting the "Saturday Chefs" series on BCTV News for more than a decade; the television station is now Global and newscasters Jennifer Mather and Jill Krop have cooked up a storm with me over the years.

I hosted one segment with Barbara-Jo MacIntosh, owner of the Books To Cooks store in Vancouver's chic Yaletown. Barbara-Jo and I started to drop fritters into what we thought was the right temperature for frying them. Much to our surprise, the oil was far too hot and started to literally "pop" like popcorn, hitting us everywhere. The cameraman kept shooting as we jumped back from the pan and belatedly realized we had the gas set on high! So watch your oil temperature whenever you do any frying of this nature.

Fritters are a favourite Mediterranean appetizer and are returning to menus in restaurants throughout North America. My mom's salmon and fresh fall corn fritters were a family favourite. You can also substitute cooked leftover salmon for the shrimp.

BATTER:

¾ cup	flour	175 mL
1 tsp	baking powder	5 mL
	salt and pepper, to taste	
¼ cup	green onions, finely chopped	60 mL
2 tbsp	parsley, finely chopped	30 mL
1	jalapeno pepper, seeded, finely chopped	1
¾ cup	beer	175 mL
1 cup	cooked baby shrimp, coarsely chopped	250 mL
1 ¼ cup	corn kernels (frozen or 2 small ears fresh)	310 mL
	shot of Tabasco	
1	egg white	1
	oil for frying, i.e. (canola, safflower)	

METHOD:

In a bowl, blend the flour, baking powder, salt and pepper. In a separate bowl, mix the onions, parsley, jalapeno pepper and beer. Gently fold into the dry ingredients. Fold in the shrimp, corn, Tabasco. In a small bowl, beat the egg white until it forms stiff peaks, then fold carefully into the batter. Can be made 2–3 hours ahead of serving, which gives a lighter batter. Refrigerate until ready to make.

Heat about 1 in/2.5 cm of oil in a deep sauté pan to a temperature of 250–275°F/120–135°C. In batches, drop about 1 tbsp/15 mL of batter at a time into the hot oil. Fry on both sides until golden brown, 3–4 minutes. Drain on paper towels. Serve immediately with assorted dips, or reheat in a 350°F/180°C oven for about 5–8 minutes or until hot and crispy. Serve with the suggested sauces.

DIPS FOR FRITTERS:

Chinese plum sauce, mango chutney, **Fresh Chive Mayonnaise** (p. 62) or **Quick Lemon Dill Mayonnaise** (pg. 63)

TO SERVE:

On each salad plate, arrange one or two fritters per person, depending on how big you make the fritters. Top each with a little Avocado Cream Sauce, then drizzle a little of the Tomato Salsa over all. Garnish the plate with a few sprigs of cilantro.

DIANE'S SECRETS:

This recipe is an adaptation of fritters we had many years ago at a San Francisco restaurant spearheaded by one of America's most talented chefs, Bradley Ogden. He now holds reign at the famous Larkspur Inn in Larkspur, California. I have also served these topped with an **Avocado Cream Sauce** (pg. 67) and **Tomato Salsa** (pg. 154) for a Santa Fe twist! Just make the fritters a little bigger and flatten to make them thinner.

BRIE AND SAINT ANDRÉ CHEESECAKE WITH MANGOES AND BERRIES

Serves 14–16 as appetizer or dessert

The marriage of the French cheeses brie and Saint André is a sinfully rich treat for festive celebrations. Serve with a glass of champagne or other sparkling wine. This cheesecake is equally delightful as an appetizer or dessert course, with champagne a choice with either. It's best made a day ahead for the cheesecake to firm up.

CRUST:

¼ cup	toasted pecans	60 mL
¼ cup	dry bread crumbs	60 mL

METHOD:

Slightly butter a 9-in/22.5-cm springform pan on bottom and sides. In a food processor, blend the pecans and bread crumbs until fine. Sprinkle the mixture on the sides and bottom of the pan to coat evenly. Shake the pan and let the excess mixture settle on the bottom. Bake in a 350°F/180°C oven for 5 minutes. Remove from oven and set aside to cool while you prepare the cheesecake filling.

CHEESECAKE FILLING:

4	large eggs	4
12 oz	solid cream cheese	300 g
¾ cup	berry sugar	175 mL
8 oz	brie cheese, rind removed	200 g
8 oz	Saint André cheese, rind removed	200 g
½ cup	sour cream	125 mL

METHOD:

In a food processor, combine the cheesecake ingredients until just smooth; don't overbeat. Pour into the prepared springform pan. Bake in a 350°F/180°C oven for 50–55 minutes, or until golden and firm on top. Cool. The cheesecake will fall and crack slightly. When completely cool, turn upside down on a serving plate. Cover with plastic wrap and refrigerate overnight.

TOPPING:

| 1 cup | mangoes, chopped and peeled | 250 mL |
| 1 cup | fresh strawberries or whole raspberries, chopped | 250 mL |

METHOD:

Just before serving, combine the fruit and sprinkle evenly over the cheesecake.

TO SERVE:

As appetizer, provide one or two cheese knives for guests to cut the cheesecake into small wedges to put on crackers or Melba toast.

For dessert, slice in thin wedges. Place on salad plates, decorate with a few grapes and pass the crackers or Melba toast.

DIANE'S SECRETS:

Equally tantalizing is using 8 oz / 200 g each of Stilton and chèvre, instead of the brie and St. André. Top with caramelized apples or pears.

CARAMELIZED APPLES OR PEARS:

In a sauté pan, melt ¼ cup / 60 ml butter; add 2 cups / 500 ml peeled, cored, thinly sliced Granny Smith apples or Bosc pears and juice of ½ lemon. Simmer on low until the apples or pears are softened, about 10 minutes. Add ¼ cup / 60 ml brown sugar and simmer for another few minutes, or until the apples or pears are caramelized. Cool, refrigerate. Just before serving, spread the apples or pears on top of the chèvre-Stilton cheesecake.

GUACAMOLE ON THE HALF SHELL

Serves 6

A new age version of the classic guacamole dip. Everyone creates his or her own Guacamole. Serve it as a first course for a southwestern menu (**Tex-Mex-Santa Fe**, pg. 17). Just make sure the avocados are perfectly ripe before you make this dish.

INGREDIENTS:

3	**ripe avocados, cut in half, pit removed**	3
1	**head leafy greens, sliced into thin strips**	1
	tortilla chips	
2	**limes, cut in quarters**	2
6 tbsp	**Mexican salsa**	90 mL
1	**large tomato (or 6 Roma tomatoes), seeded, coarsely chopped**	1
3 tbsp	**green onions, finely chopped**	45 mL
3 tbsp	**sour cream**	45 mL
	salt and pepper to taste	

METHOD:

Just before serving, place a small bed of leafy greens on 6 salad plates. Set a half avocado in the middle of the greens. Surround the greens with some tortilla chips and a lime quarter. Spoon 1 tbsp/15 mL salsa into each cavity. Sprinkle the tomatoes and onions evenly over the top of each avocado. Top each with ½ tbsp/7.5 mL sour cream. Sprinkle with a little salt and pepper. To eat, with a fork or spoon mash the guacamole ingredients with the avocado meat to make a chunky dip. Pass the tortillas and dig in! Olé!

TEQUILA-SPIKED
AVOCADO-SHRIMP COCKTAIL

Serves 4–6

Avocado glorifies this tequila-spiked shrimp cocktail, a mucho grande start to any Mexican dinner party.

11½ oz can	**Bloody Mary mix**	345 mL
⅓ cup	**tequila or vodka**	80 mL
3 tbsp	**lime juice**	45 mL
⅓ cup	**green onion,**	80 mL
	finely chopped	
⅓ cup	**cilantro, finely chopped**	80 mL
1	**jalapeno pepper, seeded,**	1
	finely chopped	
	salt and pepper to taste	
2	**ripe avocados**	2
¾ lb	**cooked baby shrimp**	300 g
	coarse or regular salt	
	(for dipping glass rims)	
	lime wedges	
	tortilla chips	

METHOD:

In a bowl, stir together the Bloody Mary cocktail mix, tequila or vodka, lime juice, onions, cilantro, jalapeno pepper, salt and pepper to taste. Pit and peel the avocados, cut into small cubes. Add the cubes and the shrimp to the cocktail mixture.

TO SERVE:

Rub the rims of 4–6 margarita or martini glasses with a lime wedge. Immediately dip rims into a dish filled with about ¼ in /.5 cm of coarse or regular salt.

Spoon avocado-shrimp equally into the glasses, pouring enough of the Bloody Mary-tequila juice to cover the avocado and shrimp. Garnish with lime wedges and serve with tortilla chips. Drink any remaining juices from the cocktail!

CILANTRO

Also known as Chinese parsley, cilantro is a member of the coriander family. Its flat green leaves have a distinctive aroma and taste and should be used sparingly. It is often used in Chinese and Mexican dishes. People either like its distinct taste or hate it.

MAUI PRAWNS WITH
MANGO-MACADAMIA NUT SALAD

Serves 4, as a salad course

While in Maui, Doug and I attended a fundraising dinner for which many of Hawaii's top chefs donated their time to present their exquisite specialities. This is my adaptation of one of the signature dishes. I found it was outstanding; hope you'll agree! It can be served equally successfully as an appetizer or salad course.

SALAD:

	mixed greens (about 1 cup/250 mL per serving)	
1	mango, peeled, thinly sliced	1
½ cup	macadamia nuts or toasted sliced almonds, coarsely chopped	125 mL
	lime wedges	

SOY-GINGER VINAIGRETTE:

2 tbsp	soy sauce	30 mL
¼ cup	fresh lime juice	60 mL
1 tbsp	shallots, finely chopped	15 mL
1 tsp	fresh ginger, finely chopped	5 mL
1	large clove garlic, crushed	1
2 tbsp	Chinese sweet chili sauce	30 mL
½ cup	peanut oil, or light salad oil	125 mL
2 tsp	pure sesame oil	10 mL
	salt and pepper to taste	

METHOD:

In a small bowl, blend the first six ingredients, then whisk in the oils slowly. Add salt and pepper to taste. Can be made a day or two ahead of serving and refrigerated.

MAUI PRAWNS:

3 tbsp	**peanut oil or salad oil**	45 mL
16–20	**medium uncooked prawns, peeled, tails left on**	16–20
½ cup	**green onions, finely chopped**	125 mL
2	**cloves garlic, finely chopped**	2
2 tbsp	**fresh ginger, finely chopped**	30 mL
2 tbsp	**Chinese oyster sauce**	30 mL
¼ tsp	**sambal oelek, or to taste**	1 mL

METHOD:

Just before serving, heat the oil in a sauté pan. Add the prawns, sauté until opaque, 2–3 minutes. Add the onions, garlic and ginger. Sauté a minute or two, then add the oyster sauce and the sambal oelek, stirring to blend. Set aside while you assemble the appetizer or salad.

TO SERVE:

Toss the mixed greens with enough of the soy-ginger vinaigrette to just coat. Add a little salt and pepper to taste. Divide evenly on 4 salad plates, mounding the salad on one half of the plate. Arrange the mango slices around the greens and sprinkle each salad with the nuts. Place the prawns on a curve on the other half of the greens, drizzling a little of the sauce over the prawns. Add a few lime wedges to each plate.

DIANE'S SECRETS:

Sambal oelek is an Indonesian red chili sauce served as a condiment or to add a kick to Asian dishes.

RAINCOAST'S NACHOS
SOUTHWESTERN STYLE

This dip was popular on my book tours, and a favourite at a reception attended by Raincoast Books sales representatives from across Canada. So for all the sales reps who have supported my cookbooks, this will always be your recipe! Serves at least 24 as an appetizer. You can halve the recipe to serve 10–12.

3 tbsp	olive oil	45 mL
1 cup	red or yellow onions, finely chopped	250 mL
4	peppers (red, yellow and orange), chopped	4
4–5	cloves garlic, finely chopped	4–5
10	small jalapeno peppers, seeded, finely chopped	10
½ tsp	crushed dried red pepper flakes, or to taste	2.5 mL
2 cups	corn niblets, fresh or frozen	500 mL
3–4 tbsp	chili powder, or to taste	45–60 mL
2–3 tbsp	cumin, or to taste	30–45 mL
	pepper to taste	
	juice of 6 small limes	
16 oz	solid cream cheese	400 g
2 cups	sour cream	500 mL
2 cups	Monterey Jack cheese, grated	500 mL

TOPPING:

2 cups	tomatoes, seeded, finely chopped	500 mL
⅓ cup	chopped cilantro	80 mL
	tortilla chips, assorted colours	

METHOD:

In a large sauté pan, heat the oil and sauté the onions, peppers, garlic, jalapeno peppers and red pepper flakes a for few minutes until slightly softened. Add the corn niblets, chili powder, cumin, pepper and lime juice, and sauté for a few minutes more to blend the spices well into the mixture.

With an electric mixer, blend the cream cheese until softened. Add the sour cream just until blended. Fold in the Monterey Jack, then add this cheese mixture to the vegetable mixture, blending well. Put in a shallow casserole dish (I use a 2-in/5-cm deep pottery casserole dish that can go from oven to table). Bake at 350°F/180°C for about 30 minutes, or until heated through. Can be made a day ahead and refrigerated. Take out at least an hour before reheating.

TO SERVE:

Just before serving, sprinkle the chopped tomatoes over the top of the dip. For cilantro fans, drizzle some chopped cilantro over the tomatoes. Provide a big bowl of tortilla chips and let everyone dig in.

KASEY WILSON'S
CRAB LEGS AND PRAWNS

Kasey Wilson is one of Canada's premier food, wine and travel writers as well as restaurant reviewer, author of several cookbooks and co-host of the Vancouver CFUN radio show *The Best of Food and Wine* with wine expert Anthony Gismondi. One of the first seafood dishes Kasey served to Doug and me was her amazing Alaska King Crab Legs and Prawns.

Be sure to order the crab legs in advance, and order the best. You want thick crabs, not thin. The fish markets do have some select ones — called "Meris" — that have more meat, so be sure to ask for them.

I like to add a Caesar or seasonal green salad to make it a meal on its own. This seafood specialty is for a very special occasion and is well worth the splurge. One word of warning: Your kitchen will smell like a fish market while the crab is roasting!

KASEY'S TIPS ON PREPARING THE CRAB AND PRAWNS:

Allow 1 or 2 large Alaska king crab legs per person, along with 3 or 4 prawns. Thaw the crab legs 2–3 hours before serving, then heat on a rack for about 8 minutes per side in a 350°F/ 180°C oven until heated through. If the prawns are raw, peel, leaving the tails intact; put into a saucepan, cover with water and bring to a boil. Simmer for about 5 minutes until the prawns turn pink. Drain; sprinkle with lemon juice and a little salt. Keep warm. Arrange the hot seafood on large platters with sauces for dipping and lots of warmed sourdough bread.

SAUCES FOR DIPPING:

I like to have two or three different dips to complement the seafood. **Quick Aioli Dip** (pg. 63), **Quick Lemon Dill Mayonnaise** (pg. 63) or **Hot Devilled Butter** (pg. 65) would be ideal dips and can be made well in advance of serving. If time is a factor, a good commercial tartar or seafood cocktail sauce would be fine.

OLIVE CHEESE BALLS

The perfect party savoury with wine or beer, I've served these for over 20 years and they still bring raves and requests for the recipe. I like to use small cocktail onions along with the olives for variety. Makes about 24 balls; I usually double this recipe to have extra on hand.

24	**small pimento-stuffed olives**	24

METHOD:

Place the olives or onions on paper towels, pat dry to absorb any liquid. Set aside.

PASTRY MIXTURE:

1 cup	**grated sharp cheddar cheese or Monterey Jack, or a combination**	250 mL
¼ cup	**soft butter**	60 mL
½ cup	**flour**	125 mL
¼ tsp	**salt**	1 mL
½ tsp	**sweet or Spanish paprika**	2.5 mL

In a medium bowl, blend the cheese and butter with your hands. Add the flour, salt and paprika, blending well to form a soft dough. Add a little more butter if the pastry seems too dry. Chill for about 15 minutes.

To make balls, flatten about 2 teaspoons of the dough in the palm of your hand. Place an olive or onion in the middle of the dough and pinch together to completely cover the olive or onion; add a little more dough if needed. Roll in the palms of your hands to form a smooth ball. Place on cookie sheet. Bake in a 400°F/200°C oven for 10–12 minutes or until golden and firm to touch. Can be made a day or two ahead of serving. Refrigerate.

TO SERVE:
Reheat in 325°F/160°C oven for 5–8 minutes, or until hot.

BAGNA CAUDA

Serves 6–8

A typical Spanish appetizer, Bagna Cauda reposes among vegetables and bread sticks for dipping. Even those who claim not to like anchovies will enjoy the dip's subtle flavour.

1 pt	**whipping cream**	475 mL
4 tbsp	**butter**	60 mL
8	**flat anchovy fillets**	8
	milk, for rinsing fillets	
1	**large clove garlic, crushed**	1
	bread sticks	
	assorted vegetables	

METHOD:

In a 4-cup/1-L enamelled casserole or saucepan, bring the cream to a boil and simmer, stirring frequently, for 30–40 minutes or until thickened: there should be about 1 cup/250 mL remaining; this stage can be done just before the guests arrive. Set the pot aside, but do not refrigerate or it will turn to butter when you reheat. Drain the anchovy fillets; rinse them in milk to eliminate some of the salt; pat dry and chop finely. Melt the butter in a chafing dish that fits over a candle, but do not allow to become brown. Add the anchovies, garlic and thickened cream, blend well until just warmed and serve at once. Keep warm over a candle.

VEGETABLE SUGGESTIONS:

Cucumbers, carrots, red or yellow peppers and celery, all cut into thin, 2-inch/5-cm strips; cherry tomatoes, zucchini, blanched asparagus spears.

TO SERVE:

Serve with bread sticks and an assortment of vegetables, prepared ahead of time and arranged on a decorative platter.

CAJUN PRAWNS WITH CREOLE TARTAR SAUCE

Serves 6 as appetizer

This is my version of the typical New Orleans Cajun spice mix and I use it as a rub for seafood, meats and poultry. As Chef Emeril puts it, "kick it up a notch" by increasing the amount of cayenne if you like it "hot, hot, hot."

Serve the prawns with the **Creole Tartar Sauce** (pg. 64).

CAJUN SPICES:

¾ cup	Hungarian or Spanish sweet paprika	175 mL
2 tbsp	cayenne	30 mL
3 tbsp	ground black pepper	45 mL
5 tbsp	garlic powder	75 mL
2 tbsp	onion salt	30 mL
1 tbsp	dried oregano	15 mL
1 tbsp	dried thyme	15 mL

METHOD:

Combine all ingredients in a small bowl and put into a sealed jar. This will keep for weeks in a dry place. Also great as a barbecue rub.

SEAFOOD:

36	medium-sized prawns, peeled, tails left on	36
4 tbsp	light olive oil or vegetable oil	60 mL
	lime wedges	
	cilantro	

METHOD:

Just before serving, heat the oil in a large fry pan. Shake the prawns with enough of the spice mix to lightly coat each piece. Sauté the prawns with more of the spice mix to lightly coat each piece. Saute for about 4 minutes, until just opaque. Decorate your serving platter with wedges of limes and cilantro, serve with **Creole Tartar Sauce** (pg. 64).

TO STORE DRY HERBS:

Never keep your dry spices near heat, and use within six months for peak flavour. Use fresh herbs in place of dry whenever you can, as the dry — especially basil and rosemary — does not compare in taste. Freshly grated nutmeg and ginger also are superior to the dried. Try the exotic Thai basil in your Asian dishes whenever available for a delicate flavour.

LISA'S SOUTHWESTERN WRAPS

Serves 2–4 as lunch, or 4 as appetizer.

Lisa Rowsan, one of Vancouver's talented young chefs, created these fabulous southwestern wraps. A hit at any party!

SANTA FE DRESSING:

½ cup	real mayonnaise	125 mL
1 tbsp	canned smoked chipotle purée	15 mL
1 ½ tsp	cumin, or to taste	7.5 mL
	juice of 2 limes or lemons	
	salt and pepper to taste	

CHICKEN FILLING:

2 cups	cooked chicken, cut in small cubes	500 mL
⅓ cup	red onions, finely diced	80 mL
½ cup	red and yellow peppers, finely chopped	125 mL
4	8-inch flour tortillas (sun-dried tomato or regular)	4
1 cup	mixed greens	250 mL
½ cup	red or yellow peppers, or a combination	125 mL

GARNISH:

Julienne the remaining peppers, set aside

METHOD:

In a small bowl, combine the dressing ingredients. Can be made a day ahead and refrigerated.

On the day of serving, in a medium bowl, combine the chicken, onions and peppers. Fold in enough dressing to bind well; save the remaining dressing. Refrigerate until ready to assemble.

TO ASSEMBLE:

Lay each tortilla flat. Spread the remaining dressing equally to cover the upper surface of each. Spread equally about a 2-in /5-cm wide strip of greens along the edge of each tortilla. Cover the greens with ½ of the chicken filling on each tortilla. Beginning at the same edge, very tightly roll up the tortillas. They must be tight, or they will fall apart when slicing. Bind each tortilla tightly with plastic wrap, twisting the ends. Refrigerate.

TO SERVE:

Slice each roll diagonally into 3–4 pieces; stand the pieces on a serving platter. Place a piece of the julienned peppers in the centre of each roll segment.

For a dramatic presentation, coarsely crush some red and blue tortilla chips and line a platter with them, then place the rolls on top.

ITALIAN BRUSCHETTA

Serves 4–6

This appetizer is always popular for any party, especially when the summer tomatoes are ripe for picking! Just multiply the ingredients accordingly. I like to add a chèvre-ricotta spread to give the bruschetta another dimension.

CROSTINIS:

1	**sourdough baguette, sliced about 1/4 in/5 mm thick**	

METHOD:

1 Place slices on a cookie sheet, toast in a 350°F/ 180°C oven for about 5 minutes on each side, or until crisp. Store in airtight container. Can be made a day ahead or on morning of serving.

TOMATO SALSA (pg. 68):

Make on morning of serving. Cover, leave at room temperature.

CHEESE SPREAD:

1 cup	**soft chèvre**	250 mL
1 cup	**creamy ricotta cheese**	250 mL
3 tbsp	**fresh basil, finely chopped**	45 mL

METHOD:

In a bowl, blend the two cheeses until creamy. Fold in the basil. Can be made a day ahead and refrigerated.

TO SERVE: Put the crostinis in a basket. Put the cheese spread in a bowl, place in the middle of a platter. Drain the tomato salsa, spoon around the bowl of cheese spread.

Let the guests spread a little of the cheese mixture on a crostini, then top with a little of the salsa.

RAND AND SUZIE'S
ROASTED BEET AND CHÈVRE TART

Serves 12–16 as appetizer first course, or 6–8 for lunch

In celebration of the new millennium, our family did a house exchange with the McNeill family on the Gold Coast of Australia. Our son Rand and daughter-in-law Suzie spent a few days in the resort town of Noosa and came back raving about this fantastic roasted beet-chèvre tart they enjoyed at one of Noosa's hottest restaurants. After much testing I came up with my own version of the tart, which received accolades from my family and friends. Roasted beets, often listed as beetroots, appear everywhere on Australian menus. It's best to serve this tart on salad plates in small wedges; decorate the plates with watercress or cilantro. For lunch, add a green side salad. This tart is rich, so slice thinly.

The sour-cream topping will be absorbed into the beet tart, giving a pale purple mosaic presentation.

TART PASTRY:

1 ¼ cups	**flour**	310 mL
½ tsp	**salt**	2.5 mL
½ cup	**chilled butter**	125 mL
2	**egg yolks**	2
¼ cup	**ice water**	60 mL

METHOD:

In a food processor, combine the flour, salt and butter until just crumbly. Add the egg yolks and water. Process until just blended. Remove and gently knead the dough a minute or two until smooth. Wrap and chill for 30 minutes, or freeze for later use. Roll pastry out to line a 10-in /25-cm flan pan; press well into bottom and up the sides, trimming the edges. Cover the pastry with parchment paper, fill with dried beans or rice. Bake in a 375°F /190°C oven for 10 minutes. Remove the beans and paper, prick the bottom of pastry with a fork. Bake, uncovered, for 10–12 minutes longer or until golden. Cool.

Rand and Suzie's Roasted Beet and Chèvre Tart > pg. 40

Maui Prawns with Mango-Macadamia Nut Salad   > pg. 31

Chicken-Mango Salsa in Lychee Nuts > pg. 44
& Vicki's Smoked Salmon and Potato Crisps with Wasabi Cream > pg. 45

New York Duck Salad with Crispy Wontons > pg. 104

Grilled Tuna Salad > pg. 100

Singaporean Spicy Asparagus with Shiitake Mushroom Sauce   > pg. 131

Oven French Fries   > *pg. 124*

TOPPING:

1 cup	**sour cream**	250 mL
1 tbsp	**Dijon mustard**	15 mL

FILLING:

8 oz	**solid cream cheese**	200 g
3 tbsp	**sour cream**	45 mL
	salt and pepper to taste	
2	**large eggs**	2
5 oz	**chèvre**	125 g
2	**large beets, roasted, pureed**	2
2 tbsp	**chives or green onions,**	30 mL
	finely chopped	

METHOD:

In a small bowl, combine the sour cream and mustard. Refrigerate while you prepare the rest of the tart.

In a food processor, combine filling ingredients and process until smooth. Should make about 3 cups /750 mL. Pour into the cooled crust and bake in a 350°F/180°C oven for 35–40 minutes, or until firm to touch in the middle. Cool for about 5 minutes, then spread the topping evenly over the tart and bake for another 5–8 minutes. Remove, cool, or serve while warm. Can be made a day ahead, cooled, refrigerated. Reheat in a 350°F/ 180°C for 20–25 minutes, or until heated through. Slice into very thin wedges and serve.

ROASTED BEETS:

Peel the beets, slice each into 8 wedges. Place in a bowl and toss with a little olive oil to coat, sprinkle with pepper and salt. Place on a slightly oiled cookie sheet and roast in a 400°F/200°C oven for 35–40 minutes, or until softened. Check frequently after 25 minutes to make sure beets don't become overcooked and dry. Puree until smooth.

JANE'S ASPARAGUS IN A PUMPKIN
WITH PEANUT DIP

Serves 6–8

Whenever we hosted a party for the Vancouver International Film Festival, the first appetizer that everyone looked for was the fresh asparagus spears standing regally in a large pumpkin, with peanut dip in a smaller pumpkin! Jane MacDonald, the festival's superb marketing expert, was always the first to start the lineup! This recipe is for you, Jane!

Forget dipping apples — serve this instead at your next Halloween party, or for any autumn affair when the pumpkins arrive from the farms.

DIP:

½ cup	chunky peanut butter	125 mL
1 tbsp	soy sauce	15 mL
1 tbsp	sesame oil	5 mL
1 tsp	lemon juice	5 mL
2	cloves garlic, pressed	2
1 tsp	sweet Chinese chili sauce	5 mL
2 tbsp	brown sugar	30 mL
½–¾ cup	plain yogurt	125–175 mL
2 tbsp	toasted sesame seeds	30 mL

METHOD:

Combine all ingredients in a food processor, adding just enough yogurt to be thick enough for dipping the asparagus. Blend just until smooth. Refrigerate up to 2 days ahead of serving. To serve, bring to room temperature and thin out with a little more yogurt if necessary.

ASPARAGUS:

36–42	asparagus spears (allow 6 per person)	36–42

On the morning of serving, trim and clean the asparagus and blanch for 2–3 minutes in a large saucepan with about an inch of boiling water until just tender-crisp. Don't overcook. Drain and chill in ice water. Pat dry and layer between paper towels on a large plate. Refrigerate until ready to serve.

PUMPKINS:

Early in the day, prepare the pumpkins: 1 large, nicely rounded pumpkin, big enough to hold asparagus, top cut off, seeded and wiped dry; 1 small pumpkin for the dip, top cut off, seeded and whipped dry. Decorate in a zigzag design around the top of the pumpkins.

DIANE'S SECRETS:

You may want to blanch more asparagus spears for the dramatic effect in the pumpkin. For the peanut dip, it's best to add just enough yogurt to make it thick. It will thicken even more in the refrigerator if made a day or two ahead of time, and you can then add a little more yogurt if it seems too thick when you're ready to serve. The dip is also great for grilled or roasted chicken breasts.

TO SERVE:

Fill the large pumpkin with the asparagus spears standing up, and fill the smaller one with the dip. Place side by side. Let everyone do their own dipping!

JUST THE FACTS — WHY IS THE ASPARAGUS ALWAYS LIMP?

Did you know that the longer asparagus has been picked, the woodier it becomes and the more wrinkled its skin? The spears should be crisp and firm, and their tips should be tightly closed. To keep the asparagus fresh, remove the elastic, put into a jug with a little water added to the bottom, and stand in the refrigerator. When ready to blanch or roast, hold the asparagus in two hands and gently bend the asparagus. It will automatically break off at the tough end of the spear. I always look for medium-thick asparagus spears, as they retain their crispness much better than the more delicate thin ones. White asparagus is really not worth the price — totally overrated! Its flavour isn't as intense and most of the time it is on its last legs in most markets.

CHICKEN - MANGO SALSA
IN LYCHEE NUTS

I came across the idea for this fun "quickie" appetizer during a trip Doug and I made to New Zealand in December 2001. We had a fabulous week with Ross and Linda Davidson and their son Fraser. Ross and Doug both retired as team physicians for the Vancouver Canucks, and shortly afterward Ross and Linda returned to Ross' native city, Auckland. We had such fun in their marvellous kitchen, with Ross acting as my "sous chef"! As we whipped up the evening dinners he spoiled us with some outstanding Kiwi wines. On one of our shopping sprees to the markets I came across a recipe brochure advertising Cointreau and vodka cocktails with assorted appetizers. This one caught my eye and once home I worked on it. Here's my version.

14 oz	can lychee nuts, well drained, bottoms thinly sliced off to lie flat, OR	350 g
1	package rice crackers black and white sesame seeds	1

FILLING:

1 cup	cooked chicken breasts, finely chopped	250 mL
1	large mango, finely chopped (about 3/4 cup/175 mL)	1
	zest and juice of 1 small lime or lemon	
1 1/2 tsp	Madras curry powder, or to taste	7.5 mL
2 tsp	fresh ginger, finely grated	10 mL
	salt and pepper to taste	
3 tbsp	cilantro, finely chopped (optional)	45 mL
	Fresh cilantro (for garnish)	

METHOD:

On the morning of serving, in a small bowl blend the filling ingredients. Stuff the lychee nuts with the filling. Top with a sprig of fresh cilantro. Refrigerate until ready to serve.

TO SERVE:

On a platter, arrange Chinese soup spoons. Evenly sprinkle on the spoons either the black or white sesame seeds to form a thin layer on the bottom of each. Arrange a stuffed lychee nut in the centre of each spoon and serve immediately.

DIANE'S SECRETS:

Rice crackers can be used in place of the lychee nuts. Put the salsa in a small bowl, surround with the rice crackers and serve.

VICKI'S SMOKED SALMON AND POTATO CRISPS WITH WASABI CREAM

Makes about 24

These fun appetizers went over well on Vicki Gabereau's special Oscar show. This is another "quickie" appetizer from New Zealand, with a teaser potato chip as the base for smoked salmon topped with a wasabi cream topping. Try the peppered candy salmon for an equally tasty bite. If you're a wasabi fan, add more to the sour cream! You may want to use half smoked salmon and half peppered salmon for a variety.

WASABI CREAM:

½ cup	**sour cream**	125 mL
1 tsp	**Japanese wasabi paste**	5 mL
	zest of lime + 1 tsp/5 mL juice	
12	**thin slices of smoked salmon, sliced in half**	12
	OR	
24	**thin slices of peppered candy salmon, sliced on the diagonal**	24
24	**small even-size salted potato chips, or Pringles fresh dill sprigs**	24

METHOD:

On the morning of serving or a day ahead, in a small bowl, blend the sour cream, wasabi paste, zest and juice of the lime. Refrigerate. Just before serving, place the chips on a large platter, arrange a piece of the salmon on top of each. Top with a little wasabi cream and a sprig of dill. Serve immediately.

TURKISH MEZE

Turkey boasts that its culinary arts rank among the top three in the world (the others being France and China), and having travelled in Turkey I can honestly say there is truth to its claim. We found the food always fresh and exciting, with lots of fresh fruits, vegetables and seafood. It was also very cheap, if you avoided the big tourist restaurants.

We were fascinated by the markets: huge sacks of spices from around the world; fresh fish from the Black Sea, barbecued right on the boats and stuffed inside fresh bread; whole lamb roasted on vertical spits; food vendors everywhere making fresh sandwiches with meats, tomatoes and cheese topped with tzatziki. Turkish bread equals France's finest: always fresh from the ovens and rushed to the stores at daybreak.

History books tell us that during the great days of the Ottoman Empire the Turkish chefs of the imperial kitchens in Topkapi Palace devoted their lives to creating new dishes to please the sultan. With 500 or so concubines and several official and unofficial wives, the sultan needed to keep up his strength; the story goes that his chefs laboured round the clock to provide him with the right foods to keep his energy up and his women happy!

Whenever you eat in Turkey you will find a meze buffet. Similar to Italian antipasto or Spanish tapas, meze are Turkish appetizers or a first course. Several small dishes are served hot or cold, for lunch or dinner, and often as meals in themselves. Serve the meze with **Moroccan Roasted Chicken** (pg. 181), **Grilled Salmon and Onions** (pg. 162) or **Barbecued Leg of Lamb** (pg. 192). I'm including recipes for a few of my most popular meze dishes. Provide a basket of pita bread and Mediterranean flat bread with the meze.

If time is a factor, choose a few items from a specialty market or deli to round out your own selection. Greek specialties such as dolmades, squid, and spanakopita also blend well with Turkish Meze.

MEZE SUGGESTIONS:

Serves 12

Tzatziki (from your deli
or make your own)
Cheese: large wedge of feta cheese
Pita bread and Mediterranean
flat bread

CHÈVRE WITH RED PEPPERS:

1 ½ cup	chèvre	375 mL	
1 tsp	olive oil	5 mL	
1	red pepper, finely chopped	1	
1	clove garlic, pressed	1	
1 tsp	brown sugar	5 mL	
1 tsp	white or sherry vinegar	5 mL	
	pinch cumin		

METHOD:

In a skillet, heat the olive oil. Add the chopped red peppers and garlic, sauté for few minutes. Add the rest of the ingredients and simmer for 2–3 minutes. Cool.

In a small ramekin or serving dish, mound the chèvre, sprinkle the red pepper mixture over the chèvre and serve with pita bread and Mediterranean flat bread.

ANNETTE'S MEDITERRANEAN
VINAIGRETTE DRESSING FOR VEGETABLE MEZE:

½ cup	white wine vinegar	125 mL	
½ tbsp	cumin	7.5 mL	
3	cloves garlic, pressed	3	
3 tbsp	Spanish or Hungarian paprika	45 mL	
	salt and pepper to taste		
¾ cup	vegetable oil	175 mL	

METHOD:

In a bowl, whisk the ingredients to blend well, adding the oil slowly at the end. Can be made several days ahead. Refrigerate.

EGGPLANT DIP:

This dip or spread can be made a day or two ahead of serving.

3	medium eggplants	3	
8	cloves garlic, peeled	8	
½ tsp	cumin	2.5 mL	
1 tsp	lemon juice	5 mL	
3–4 tbsp	Annette's Mediterranean Vinaigrette Dressing (p. 47)	45–60 mL	

METHOD:

Wash eggplants, make four incisions in each and insert the garlic cloves. Bake on a cookie sheet at 450°F/230°C for about 40 minutes or until soft and tender. Peel and mash eggplant pulp, removing most of the seeds (they tend to be bitter). Add cumin and lemon juice. Mix in vinaigrette dressing and check seasonings. Refrigerate. To serve, spread on pita or thin slices of French bread.

SPICED BEETS:

4 lb	fresh beets	1.8 kg
¼ cup	Annette's Mediterranean Vinaigrette Dressing (p. 47)	60 mL

METHOD:

Cover beets with water, bring to a boil and cook until tender. Drain, put into a bowl of cold water and slip off the skins. Cut beets in uniform slices. Add vinaigrette dressing to coat well, refrigerate overnight. This will keep for several days. Toss just before serving, adding more dressing if needed.

SPICED CARROTS :

1 lb	carrots, peeled and sliced 1/4 in/1 cm thick	450 g
3 tbsp	Annette's Mediterranean Vinaigrette Dressing (p. 47)	45 mL

METHOD:

Blanch the carrots for a few minutes, until slightly crunchy — don't overcook! Drain and cool. Add vinaigrette dressing, coat well. Refrigerate a day or two ahead of serving; add a little more vinaigrette if necessary before serving.

MARINATED CUCUMBERS WITH FETA:

1	large cucumber, scored lengthwise with a fork	1
1 cup	feta, crumbled	250 mL
½ cup	fresh mint, chopped	125 mL
6 tbsp	olive oil	90 mL
	zest of 1 lemon, finely chopped	
3 tbsp	lemon juice	45 mL
	salt and pepper to taste	

METHOD:

Slice the cucumbers paper-thin, saving several to stand up around the serving bowl. Pat all the slices dry between paper towels. In a bowl, toss most of the slices with the rest of the ingredients, surround with the remaining cucumber slices. Refrigerate until ready to serve. Serve on pita or Mediterranean bread, or as a side dish.

Drinks

CICADA COOLER

Serves 1

This tropical drink from the award-winning Cicada Restaurant in Sydney, Australia, definitely packs a punch! With a dynamic trio of citron vodka, Cointreau and champagne, finished off with a splash of OJ, mango purée and a twist of lime, you have the makings of a fun party ahead.

1 oz	**citron vodka**	30 mL	METHOD:
1 oz	**Cointreau**	30 mL	In a blender combine the vodka, Cointreau, orange
	splash of orange juice		and lime juice, mango purée and a few ice cubes.
	splash of lime juice		Blend until smooth. Pour into a cocktail, wine or
¼ cup	**puréed mango**	60 mL	champagne flute. Top with a little champagne, stir.
	(or strawberries, raspberries)		Place a thin slice of lime on the rim of the glass and
5	**ice cubes**	5	serve.
	champagne or other sparkling wine		
	slice of lime		

SANGRIA BLANCA

Serves 6

A lighter version of the classic Spanish drink, this is made with white wine and citrus fruit to enhance your summertime "happy hour"!

1	2 L bottle of dry white wine	1
1 cup	orange liqueur (such as Cointreau, Grand Marnier)	250 mL
½ cup	white sugar	125 mL
1	each of lime, orange, lemon, each thinly sliced	1
3	nectarines or peaches, thinly sliced	3
1	750 mL bottle lemon or club soda	1

METHOD:

Several hours before serving, combine all ingredients except the soda and refrigerate. Add soda when ready to serve, pour into wine goblets with crushed ice and some of the fruit.

THE REGAL PRINCESS
LOVEBOAT COCKTAIL

In the fall of 2001, Doug and I were invited by Helen Pinkam, vice-president western Canada for Giants Travel, to host their 35-day "Select Traveller" Royal Princess cruise from Bangkok to Sydney, Australia. This included 17 ports. We were delighted, to say the least! "Giants Select" is an elite group of travel counsellors within Giants, with its "team" of 2,000 travel professionals. "Select Travel" is a club that the Giants Select agent has established to express appreciation for their clients, and our group from across Canada was fantastic! We presented our lifestyle seminar to them between ports. Steve Britton, assistant food and beverage manager-bars, arranged the Giants Select cocktail receptions for our group and when I asked him what would be the signature cocktail of the Princess fleets, he exclaimed, "What else could it be but The Loveboat!" Steve's home, when he's not on the *Princess*, is in Huddersfield, England. He's been sailing with the Princess ships for eight years, so he truly knows his drinks. The Loveboat will put you in a mellow, sensuous mood — guaranteed! Are you ready for this?

1 oz	**melon liqueur**	30 mL	METHOD:
½ oz	**blue curaçao**	15 mL	Blend the pina colada mix with ice until smooth.
3 ½ oz	**pina colada mix**	105 mL	Half fill the glass with pina colada mix.
	(pineapple-coconut cream mix)		
5	ice cubes	5	Pour the melon liqueur down the side of the glass. Top up the glass with more pina colada mix. Float the blue curaçao on top.

GARNISH:

Pineapple and cherry. The rim of the glass is coated with shredded coconut.

SINGAPORE
SLING

Serves 1

Singapore was founded by Sir Stamford Raffles, who persuaded the Sultan of Jahore to cede the undeveloped island of Singapore to the East India Company in 1819. The city grew up along its river and harbour. Today, junks and sampans have largely given way to supertankers, freighters and passenger liners, but weekend cricket matches and the venerable Raffles Hotel keep the ambiance of the British colonial era alive. The hotel, established in 1887, is one of the few remaining great 19th-century hotels in Asia and was designated a national monument in 1987.

The Singapore Sling cocktail was originally created at the Raffles Hotel by bartender Ngiam Tong Boon. In the hotel's museum, visitors may view the safe in which Mr. Ngiam locked away his precious recipe books, as well as the Sling recipe hastily jotted down on a bar chit in 1936 by a visitor to the hotel who asked the waiter for it. Originally the Singapore Sling was meant as a woman's drink, hence the attractive pink colour. Today it is very definitely a drink enjoyed by all. Authors such as Somerset Maugham and Noel Coward once graced the bars at Raffles to enjoy their Singapore Slings. Multiply the ingredients as you wish.

1 oz	gin	30 mL
1 tbsp	cherry brandy, or cherry syrup from bottled cherries	15 mL
½ cup	pineapple juice	125 mL
1 tbsp	lime juice	15 mL
2 tsp	Cointreau	10 mL
2 tsp	Dom Benedictine or other brandy	10 mL
2 tsp	grenadine	10 mL
	dash of Angostura Bitters	

METHOD:

Blend and pour over ice cubes. Garnish with a slice of pineapple and a cherry.

MILLION DOLLAR COCKTAIL

Serves 1

All it takes to relive the intrigue of the old East is your first sip of a Million Dollar Cocktail at one of the Raffles Hotel's bars. Once as popular as the Singapore Sling, like it the Million Dollar Cocktail was an invention of Raffles Hotel bartender Ngiam Tong Boon around the early 1900s. The Million Dollar Cocktail gained considerable notoriety — and considerable sales for the Raffles Hotel — when it was featured in one of Somerset Maugham's most famous barside tales, "The Letter." Raffles Hotel has immortalized one of Maugham's great stories by continuing to serve this tangy, bittersweet creation.

2 tbsp	**gin**	30 mL	METHOD:
2 tsp	**sweet vermouth**	10 mL	Blend well and serve over ice cubes.
2 tsp	**dry vermouth**	10 mL	
½ cup	**pineapple juice**	125 mL	
	dash of egg white		
	dash of Angostura Bitters		

ROSÉ WINE WITH PINEAPPLE

Serves 4–6

This summertime drink could also be served as a light dessert! It's unique with its infusion of a few leaves of fresh basil with the wine, topped with sweet pineapple. The taste is totally soothing to the palate.

1	bottle of rosé wine, well chilled	1
1	pineapple, peeled, cored, sliced into small cubes	1
2 tbsp	berry sugar	30 mL
10	fresh basil leaves, torn in half	10

METHOD:

Several hours before serving, in a bowl toss the pineapple with the sugar and torn basil leaves. Refrigerate.

TO SERVE:

Into each wine glass, spoon several cubes of the pineapple and pieces of the basil. Pour the rosé into each glass to cover the pineapple. Nibble on the pineapple as you enjoy the refreshing chilled rosé.

FROSTED CHERRIES WITH ROSÉ BRUT OR SPARKLING SHIRAZ

Serves 4–6

Remember Mateus, the rosé party wine of the 1970s? Well, the rosé wines are making a comeback! Always popular in France for summertime entertaining, they are crisp and refreshing. Try serving a Rhone dry rosé with smoked salmon, olives and tapenades. When the summer cherries are at their peak, combine them with a sweeter rosé from the Loire region to serve as an aperitif or dessert.

2	**large egg whites**	2
1 cup	**berry sugar**	250 mL
½ lb	**whole cherries, stems on**	225 g
1	**bottle well-chilled rosé, preferably French, rosé Brut or sparkling shiraz**	1

METHOD:

On the morning of serving, with an electric mixer beat the egg whites until soft peaks begin to form. Set aside.

Place the sugar in a small bowl. Dip the cherries one at a time into the egg whites, then roll into the sugar to coat well. Place on a cookie sheet lined with parchment paper. Leave at room temperature until ready to serve.

DIANE'S SECRETS:

For dessert, add a small scoop of cherry sorbet or ice cream to the bottom of the wine goblet before topping with the cherries and the sparkling wine.

TO SERVE: Put several cherries in each wine goblet. Pour about 2 inches of the sparkling champagne or wine into the goblets, leaving the cherries slightly covered. Serve immediately.

Condiments
Sauces and
Salsas

ts,

d

STOCK MARKET'S
FRESH CHIVE MAYONNAISE

This fresh mayonnaise is hard to beat. It's one of the many fine recipes of George and Joanne Lefevbre, owners of the Stock Market at Granville Island in Vancouver. From early-morning porridge with all the trimmings to fresh soups ready for the lunch crowd, the Stock Market is a popular destination. You can pick up soups, stocks, sauces and chutneys, condiments and dressings and many other delectables. Their turkey gravy is outstanding. I must confess, I don't bother with all the last-minute fuss of making my own gravy when we have the Stock Market's!

2	egg yolks	2	METHOD:
¼ cup	fresh chives, finely minced	60 mL	Combine all ingredients except the oil in a
2 tbsp	lemon juice	30 mL	blender, mixer or food processor and blend well.
1 tbsp	Dijon mustard	15 mL	Add the oil a few drops at a time while continuing
1 tbsp	shallots, minced	15 mL	to blend until creamy. Will keep in the refrigerator
1 tsp	sea salt	5 mL	for 2–3 days.
1 tsp	white pepper	5 mL	
1 ½ cups	sunflower oil	375 mL	

S A L T

Sea salt is the best salt you can use. My favourites are Fleur de Sel from France and Maldon from England. Sea salt flavours your food in a natural way, without any artificial additives. If you can get your hands on the famous pink-coloured volcanic salt from Maui, it's sensational! Another famous salt is from England, named Maldon Sea Salt and hand-harvested at Maldon, Essex. Its package states: "With pure sea salts you eliminate the bitter after-taste with other salts and salt substitutes." Once you use sea salts you will never use any other variety. You may pay more, but you use less to bring out the flavours of dish ingredients.

QUICK LEMON DILL MAYONNAISE

Makes about 1 cup/250 mL

When time is short, start with your favourite bottled mayonnaise and add the seasonings. Do not use Miracle Whip! This mayonnaise goes well with smoked salmon, **Shrimp and Corn Fritters** (pg. 25), grilled seafood, sandwiches and so on. The Quick Aioli Dip here is equally tasty using a commercial mayonnaise as its base.

1 cup	**real mayonnaise**	250 mL	METHOD:
½ tsp	**Dijon mustard**	2.5 mL	In a small bowl, combine all the ingredients. Will
2 tbsp	**lemon juice**	30 mL	keep in the refrigerator for 2–3 days.
3 tbsp	**fresh dill, finely chopped**	45 mL	
2 tbsp	**small capers (optional)**	30 mL	
	salt and pepper to taste		

QUICK AIOLI DIP:

Add 1 large clove garlic, crushed; eliminate the fresh dill. Try roasted garlic for a sweet taste. I usually add 2–3 roasted garlic cloves to the 1 cup of mayonnaise to bring out the roasted flavour.

ROASTED GARLIC:

Toss 6 peeled cloves of garlic with a little olive oil. Wrap in tinfoil and roast in a 350°F / 180°C oven for about 30 minutes, or until softened. If the cloves are small they will roast more quickly, so check after 20 minutes.

CREOLE TARTAR SAUCE

Makes about 1 cup/250 mL

The perfect marriage with any Cajun dish, especially the **Cajun Prawns** (pg. 37) and any grilled chicken or seafood.

CREOLE TARTAR SAUCE:

1 cup	**real mayonnaise**	250 mL
1 tbsp	**grainy Dijon mustard**	15 mL
2	**cloves garlic, pressed**	2
2 tbsp	**parsley, finely chopped**	30 mL
3 tbsp	**green onions,**	45 mL
	finely chopped	
	good pinch Cajun spices, to taste	
	(see Cajun Prawns)	
	salt and pepper to taste	

METHOD:

In a small bowl, combine all ingredients. Store in refrigerator. Best made a day ahead, though will keep in refrigerator for 3–4 days.

HOT DEVILLED BUTTER

Makes about ½ cup / 125 mL

The warm piquant dip is ideal for **Kasey Wilson's Crab Legs and Prawns** presentation (pg. 34). Provide individual small dipping dishes for each of your guests.

½ cup	**butter**	125 mL	METHOD:
2 tsp	**Dijon mustard**	10 mL	In a small saucepan, melt the butter over low heat
1 tsp	**Worcestershire sauce**	5 mL	and add the rest of the ingredients, blending well.
2 tbsp	**chili sauce**	30 mL	Can be prepared a day ahead. Put in a small bowl,
	dash of Tabasco		refrigerate.
4 tsp	**lemon or lime juice,**	20 mL	
	or a combination		TO SERVE:
1 tbsp	**parsley, finely chopped**	15 mL	Heat in a small saucepan just before serving.
1	**clove garlic, pressed**	1	Divide evenly among individual dipping dishes.

SOY-HONEY
DIPPING SAUCE

Light dipping sauce for **Princely Prawns** (pg. 158) and any grilled seafood.

½ cup	**soy sauce**	125 mL	METHOD:
1 ½ tbsp	**honey**	20 mL	In a small saucepan, combine all the ingredients.
1 tbsp	**Chinese sweet chili sauce**	15 mL	Simmer over medium heat, stirring for a few
2 in	**piece fresh ginger, peeled,**	5 cm	minutes to combine the flavours. Can be made a
	finely shredded		day or two ahead. Refrigerate.
2 tbsp	**toasted sesame seeds**	30 mL	

AVOCADO CREAM SAUCE

Great as a dipping sauce for **Lisa's Southwestern Wraps** (pg. 38) or the **Shrimp and Corn Fritters** (pg. 25)

1	large ripe avocado, pitted	1	**METHOD:**
1 tbsp	lemon juice	15 mL	Just before serving, scoop out the avocado meat
1 tbsp	sour cream	15 mL	and chop coarsely. In a food processor, blend
	dash of Tabasco		all the ingredients until just smooth. Serve
	salt and pepper to taste		immediately.

JUST THE FACTS — THE AVOCADO

The best avocados you can buy are the Haas variety. One rule of thumb for buying an avocado is that it has to be ripe! How many times have we arrived home to make the perfect guacamole only to find the avocados black inside, mushy and tasteless, or still hard as rocks? To find the perfect avocado, first test by pressing gently at the narrow stem end. The flesh should give slightly. Another test is to remove the little pit stem — if the avocado meat underneath shows bright green, it's ripe; if it's black, it will be black throughout the avocado. Everyone asks, "What are you doing?" as I gently "pick" out the little tip, but it works 99.9% of the time — and don't you want the perfect avocado? In case every store has nothing but hard avocados just when you need them, pick up a few hard avocados several days ahead and leave them on the counter to ripen.

TOMATO SALSA

Quick to make, this salsa can top **Italian Bruschetta** (pg. 39), **omelettes** (pg. 152) or **fritters** (pg. 25), or be tossed with pasta.

1 cup	tomatoes, seeded, coarsely chopped	250 mL
1	clove garlic, pressed	1
¼ cup	green onions, finely chopped	60 mL
3 tbsp	fresh basil, finely chopped	45 mL
1 tsp	balsamic vinegar	5 mL
2 tbsp	olive oil	30 mL
	salt and pepper to taste	

METHOD:

In the morning or several hours before serving, combine all the ingredients in a bowl; cover and let sit at room temperature. Just before serving, drain to eliminate the extra juices.

JUST THE FACTS: THE TOMATO

The tomato was introduced to the early Spanish explorers by the Central American natives who cultivated it, and was known as a fruit, or "love apple." Fruit or vegetable, the tomato flavour depends on several factors — acidity, sugar and water content, texture of the flesh and when it is harvested. There are hundreds of varieties of tomatoes, ranging in colour from green, red, pink, yellow, orange and even brown, purple and zebra-striped! Plum tomatoes are best for roasting and sauces and have good flavour throughout the year. As every Italian will tell you, "Never put the tomatoes in the refrigerator – NEVER!" Their flavour deteriorates rapidly and they become pulpy. Let them ripen at room temperature.

Soups

STRAWBERRIES 'N CHAMPAGNE SOUP

Serves 6

When the strawberry season is at its peak, try this delightfully refreshing chilled soup to start off a summer luncheon or evening of dining. The berries must be sweet and juicy.

3 cups	**strawberries**	750 mL
½ cup	**champagne or**	125 mL
	other sparkling wine	

GARNISH:

honey yogurt and fresh mint

METHOD:

Purée the strawberries well, strain and chill. Refrigerate. Just before serving, add enough champagne to give the strawberries a tang without making the mixture too thin. Serve in individual glass bowls embedded in larger bowls of crushed ice. Garnish each with a dollop of honey-sweetened or vanilla yogurt and a sprig of mint. Servings should be small — ⅓–½ cup/80–125 mL.

CHILLED
MELON SOUP

Serves 4

Melons are one of the healthiest, most nutritious of fruits and low in calories: half a melon contains only 60 calories. I like to use purées of both honeydew and cantaloupe melons and pour them into the bowls in a yin-yang fashion. Serve this refreshing summer soup well chilled.

1	large ripe honeydew melon, chilled	1
	zest of 1 lime, finely chopped	
2 tsp	lime juice	10 mL
½–1 tsp	fresh mint, to taste, finely chopped	2.5–5 mL
1	large ripe cantaloupe melon, chilled	1
	zest of half a lemon, finely chopped	
1 tsp	lemon juice	5 mL
	fresh mint sprigs for garnish	

METHOD:

The day ahead or on the morning of serving, peel and seed both melons and cut into large cubes. Combine the honeydew with the zest of lime, lime juice and mint and mix well in a blender or food processor. Pour into a small pitcher and refrigerate. Repeat with the cantaloupe, zest of lemon and lemon juice and refrigerate in a separate pitcher.

TO SERVE:

Set out four individual-size clear glass bowls. Pour small, equal amounts of the two melon mixtures at the same time, using both hands, so that one half is the honeydew mixture and the other half the cantaloupe mixture for a yin-yang effect. Garnish each bowl with a mint sprig. Additional finely chopped melon can be put into the soup if desired.

INDONESIAN
SQUASH SOUP

Serves 10–12

Flavours come alive here with the Indonesian spices, fresh ginger and lime juice to balance the sweetness of the butternut squash. This is one of my most-requested soup recipes.

SPICE:

1 ½ tbsp	**coriander seeds**	20 mL
1 ½ tbsp	**turmeric**	20 mL
1 ½ tbsp	**ground cumin**	20 mL
1 ½ tbsp	**Madras curry powder**	20 mL
¼ tsp	**dried red chili pepper flakes**	1 mL

METHOD:

In a small chopper, grind the coriander seeds, then blend with the rest of the spices. Set aside.

C U R R Y   P O W D E R

Widely available, the best is found in specialty or Indian food stores. Experiment to find a blend that you like: start with a mild mix and work toward a stronger Madras curry. Thai blends and Sharwoods are excellent.

SOUP:

3 tbsp	olive or vegetable oil	45 mL
4	medium white onions, coarsely chopped	4
6	cloves garlic, finely chopped	6
3 tbsp	fresh ginger, grated or minced	45 mL
	salt and pepper to taste	
48 oz	can V-8 juice	1.5 L
	spice mixture	
28 oz	water	840 mL
6	14 oz/420 mL cans coconut milk	6
7 cups	butternut squash, peeled, cut into 1-in/2.5-cm cubes	1.75 L
5 cups	spinach, coarsely chopped	1.25 L
	juice of 3-4 limes, or to taste	

METHOD:

In a large soup pot, heat the olive or vegetable oil and sauté the onions and garlic a few minutes. Add the ginger, salt and pepper and continue to sauté until the onions are softened. Add the V-8 juice, water and the spice mixture and simmer for about 5 minutes, stirring to coat the vegetables with the spices. Stir in the coconut milk and add the squash. Gently simmer uncovered for about 40 minutes, or until the squash is tender. Taste for seasoning, add more spices if desired. Cool. Refrigerate.

Just before serving, chop the spinach and add to the soup along with the lime juice to taste. Add a little more V-8 juice and water if it seems too thick. Best made a day or two ahead of serving. Any leftovers freeze well.

NEW MEXICO
CORN CHOWDER

Serves 12–16

I have made tons of this soup for our athletes after cross-country competitions and track meets, and for entertaining on ski weekends. It's a meal in itself. For those who go for the really hot stuff, add more chili powder and Tabasco, or fresh chili peppers. Serve with **The Clement Family Cornbread** (pg. 200).

3 tbsp	olive or vegetable oil	45 mL
1	each red, yellow and orange peppers, julienned	1
3	onions, in small slices	3
4–5	cloves garlic, finely chopped	4–5
2	6 ½ oz / 195 mL cans green chilies, chopped	2
8 cups	V-8 juice	2 L
5	10 oz / 300 mL cans tomato soup	5
2	28 oz / 840 mL cans plum tomatoes, coarsely chopped	2
5 cups	frozen corn niblets, or a mixture of frozen and canned	1.25 L
3–4 tbsp	ground cumin	45–60 mL
3–4 tbsp	chili powder	45–60 mL
	salt and pepper to taste	
	a few shots of Tabasco, to taste	
2 tbsp	Worcestershire sauce	30 mL

TOPPING FOR SOUP:

Tortilla chips, coarsely broken

Monterey Jack cheese, grated

METHOD:

In a large stock pot, heat the oil and sauté the peppers, onions and garlic until softened and caramelized, 10 –15 minutes. Add the rest of the ingredients and simmer for 30 minutes to 1 hour. Add more V-8 juice and tomato soup if it seems too thick. Best made a day ahead.

TO SERVE:

Pour into soup bowls, sprinkle some tortilla chips and cheese on top.

GARY'S THAI CHICK PEA SOUP

Makes about 4 quarts / 4 litres

Gary Thompson, who plays a mean saxophone, moved to Vancouver from Toronto after a successful run with his own café. He is as talented in the computer world as he is in the kitchen: His Thai Chick Pea Soup is sensational! Like most restaurant recipes, it makes tons. You can cut this recipe in half if you wish. It freezes well, so you might as well go for the whole recipe while you're at it!

3 tbsp	olive oil	45 mL
4	onions, coarsely chopped	4
6	cloves garlic, finely chopped	6
3	28 oz /840 mL cans chopped tomatoes, with juice	3
3	19 oz /570 mL cans chick peas, drained	3
7	13 1/2 oz /405 mL cans coconut milk	7
	juice of 4 limes	
2 tbsp	Madras curry powder, or to taste	30 mL
2 tbsp	ground cumin, or to taste	30 mL
	salt and pepper to taste	

METHOD:

In a large soup pot, sauté the onions and garlic in the oil until golden, about 15 minutes. Add the remaining ingredients and simmer for about 30 minutes, stirring frequently. Cool and refrigerate. Best made a day or two ahead. If the soup appears too thick, add a little vegetable stock or water.

GAZPACHO WITH
AVOCADO AND CRAB

Serves 6

When the Dungeness crabs appear at our local fish markets, I like to "gussy up" the classic Spanish gazpacho. It's a sublime summertime soup course that always brings comments, and the flavours are sensational.

GAZPACHO:

2	large tomatoes	2
14 oz	can tomatoes, including juice	420 mL
½	red onion	½
½	English cucumber	½
1	red pepper, seeded	1
2	sprigs parsley	2
1	clove garlic, crushed	1
1	small jalapeno pepper, seeded, finely chopped	1
1 cup	tomato juice	250 mL
2 tbsp	Heinz chili sauce	30 mL
	juice of 1 lime	
2 tbsp	sherry vinegar	30 mL
	salt and pepper to taste	

METHOD:

At least 2–3 days ahead of serving, cut the fresh and canned tomatoes, onion, cucumber and pepper into chunks. Combine all ingredients in a food processor, a portion at a time and with an on/off rhythm, until the mixture is smooth rather than chunky. Cover and refrigerate until ready to serve.

AVOCADO TOPPING:

3	ripe avocados, peeled, seeded, mashed	3
1 tsp	lime juice	5 mL
	shot of Tabasco	
	salt and pepper to taste	

CRAB TOPPING:

1 cup	fresh Dungeness crabmeat	250 mL
1 tbsp	mayonnaise	15 mL
1 tsp	lemon juice	5 mL
	salt and pepper to taste	

GARNISH:

½	each red and yellow peppers, finely diced	½
¼ cup	chives or green onions, finely chopped	60 mL
	cilantro sprigs	
2	limes, cut into small wedges	2

TO SERVE:

Pour some of the gazpacho into 6 soup bowls. Mound a little of the mashed avocado mixture in the centre of each bowl. Top the avocado with an equal amount of the crab mixture. Sprinkle a little of the peppers and onions over the crab. Add a sprig of cilantro and serve. Pass the lime wedges.

Salads *and* Salad Dressings

ROASTED ASPARAGUS- BOCCONCINI SALAD

Serves 2

My daughter Jennifer and I had fun presenting this salad on the Vancouver Global TV "Saturday Chefs" series. We were also highlighting the Vancouver Sun Run and the Vancouver Playhouse International Wine Festival; both spectacular events are held in April. Jennifer and I enjoy taking part in the 10K Sun Run, then look forward to a fun week of the wine festival's tastings and gala dinner. The festival is recognized as one of the best internationally.

ASPARAGUS SALAD:

12	spears asparagus, trimmed of woody ends	12
1 tbsp	olive oil	15 mL
	salt and pepper to taste	
4	small balls fresh bocconcini or mozzarella, sliced into wedges	4
8	cherry tomatoes, sliced in half	8

METHOD:

Preheat the oven to 400°F/200°C. Place the asparagus on an oven tray, drizzle with the olive oil, season with salt and pepper. Place in the oven and roast for 8–10 minutes, or until the asparagus is slightly tender. Set aside to cool. Can be roasted early on the morning of serving and left at room temperature.

JUST THE FACTS—WHAT IS MOZZARELLA AND WHAT IS BOCCONCINI CHEESE?

The best mozzarella is made from whole buffalo milk and is very difficult to find in the cheese shops, and is more expensive, but well worth it when you come across it. Fresh mozzarella has a thin rind, creamy centre, and comes in a small egg shape, as well as in bite-sized shapes that are called bocconcini. Most bocconcini is made from cow's milk. It's best eaten at room temperature, and must be eaten within three to four days of purchasing. Keep the bocconcini covered with water in a container in the refrigerator. The added bonus is that it's low in fat! There is nothing like a Tomato Bocconcini Salad with slices of perfectly ripe tomatoes, thin slices of bocconcini, finely sliced purple onions topped with slivers of fresh basil and drizzled with a basic **Balsamic Vinaigrette** (pg. 107).

PANCETTA-
BLACK OLIVE VINAIGRETTE:

4	**thin slices pancetta, finely chopped**	4
2 tbsp	**shallots, finely chopped**	30 mL
1	**clove garlic, finely chopped**	1
8	**kalamata olives, pitted, coarsely chopped**	8
2 tbsp	**red wine vinegar**	30 mL
1 tbsp	**mixed fresh herbs (such as parsley, basil, oregano)**	15 mL
¼ cup	**olive oil**	60 mL
	salt and pepper to taste	

DIANE'S SECRETS:

The combination of asparagus, bocconcini and cherry tomatoes with its unusual pancetta and kalamata olive vinaigrette is unique. Pancetta can be found in Italian delis; you can also substitute prosciutto or bacon. If desired, you can blanch the asparagus for about 2 minutes. Drain, place in a bowl of ice water to cool, pat dry. Refrigerate until ready to assemble.

METHOD:

In a small fry pan, sauté the pancetta, shallots and garlic over low heat, stirring until the pancetta is crispy. In a small bowl, whisk together the pancetta mixture with the remaining vinaigrette ingredients, slowly whisking in the olive oil. Refrigerate. Just before serving, place in a small fry pan, reheat to melt the olive oil. Set aside while you prepare the salad.

TO SERVE:

On 2 salad plates, stack the asparagus. Arrange the bocconcini and cherry tomatoes around the asparagus. Drizzle the vinaigrette over all. Serve with sourdough baguette to soak up the dressing. For a delicate presentation, peel the asparagus tips before blanching. I multiply the ingredients for a summer buffet platter to complement barbecued fish or meats.

SALADE
ST.-TROPEZ

Serves 6

Doug and I, with our friend Sharon Woyat, had an exciting time wandering through the French seaside resort of St.-Tropez during our stay in Provence. We hit the Saturday morning market, which everyone told us was one of the best in France. We were not disappointed. The farmers' stalls were laden with fresh local produce, amazing cheeses, olive oils and vinegars, meats and seafoods. Artists and craftspeople sold their artwork and linen tableware. Musicians played in the small family bistros scattered throughout the market.

The bistro we chose for lunch featured its specialty salad of the day, an unusual combination of perfectly ripe cantaloupe melons, juicy cherry tomatoes and bocconcini so fresh that it melted in our mouths.

Add grilled chicken or **Chicken Breasts Supreme** (pg. 173) and baguettes, complemented with a French wine of your choice. You will feel you are experiencing the "joie de vivre" of a French market, as we did!

BASIL VINAIGRETTE DRESSING:			METHOD:
8	fresh basil leaves, finely chopped	8	Three or four days ahead of serving, in a food processor blend the chopped basil, mustard,
2 tsp	Dijon mustard	10 mL	vinegar, salt and pepper until smooth. Remove
¼ cup	sherry vinegar or white wine vinegar	60 mL	from processor and place in a small bowl. Whisk in the olive oil in a thin stream until creamy.
	salt and pepper to taste		Refrigerate. Bring to room temperature an hour
1 cup	olive oil	250 mL	or so before serving; shake well before using.

SALAD:		
1	**ripe cantaloupe melon**	1
2 cups	**small cherry tomatoes**	500 mL
2 cups	**fresh bocconcini**	500 mL
12–15	**fresh basil leaves, julienned**	12–15

METHOD:

On the day of serving, carve out the melon and bocconcini into small balls with a melon baller. Arrange the melon and bocconcini balls on a serving platter with the cherry tomatoes. Drizzle enough of the vinaigrette to lightly coat the salad. Decorate with the fresh basil leaves. Refrigerate for 30 minutes before serving.

——— T O   S T O R E   F R E S H   H E R B S ———

Fresh herbs will keep for up to a week in the fridge. Some such as parsley and cilantro can be treated like flowers, put into a glass of water, covered with a plastic bag and refrigerated. Others such as basil, rosemary and thyme should be patted dry, wrapped in paper towels and stored in plastic bags in the vegetable compartment of your refrigerator. Or chop the herbs, place about 1 tbsp / 15 mL into an ice cube compartment, fill with water and freeze; store the frozen herb cubes in plastic bags. The herbs will turn black, but the flavour will remain for months. Pop the frozen cubes into soups, stocks or marinades.

SANTA FE CHICKEN WITH
JALAPENO CREAM DRESSING

Serves 6–8

Quick to prepare, with plenty of southwestern flavours to entice your taste buds, this salad is sure to please! Works well for lunch or a light summer-evening salad. I like to serve a combination of yellow, blue and red tortilla chips with it.

JALAPENO CREAM DRESSING:

2 cups	sour cream	500 mL
1 cup	mayonnaise	250 mL
2–3 tbsp	cumin powder, to taste	30–45 mL
	juice of 2–3 large limes	
2–3	jalapenos, seeded, finely chopped	2–3

METHOD:

In a medium bowl, combine all the dressing ingredients until smooth. Can be made a day or two ahead and refrigerated.

SALAD:

4 cups	cooked chicken, cubed	1 L
1	small red onion, thinly sliced	1
2 cups	Monterey Jack cheese, shredded	500 mL
4 oz	can chopped green chilies	120 mL
	OR	
¼ cup	fresh jalapenos, seeded, finely chopped	60 mL
½ bunch	cilantro, stems removed, chopped	½ bunch
¾–1 cup	black olives, pitted	175–250 mL
1	red pepper, julienned	1
1	yellow pepper, julienned	1
1–2 heads	romaine lettuce, shredded, or mixed greens	1–2 heads
6	Roma tomatoes, cut into quarters	6
	tortilla chips for garnish	

METHOD:

In a large bowl, toss all of the salad ingredients with enough dressing to make a creamy salad, leaving out the lettuce, tomatoes and tortillas. Line a platter with the lettuce and top with the chicken mixture. Garnish with the tomato wedges, serve with a basket of tortilla chips.

For individual servings, line salad bowls with the romaine lettuce, top with some of the salad, garnish with the tomato wedges and a few tortilla chips.

JILL'S CHICKEN AND WATERMELON SALAD

Serves 4

Jill Krop, former host of the *Global Weekend News*, is now hosting the Global weekly late-night news hour. She was so much fun to work with when she hosted my segment on the "Saturday Chefs" series and many people I meet throughout the province ask, "Is she as nice as she appears on the news?" My reply is, "She sure is!" I miss doing our Saturday segments together.

This salad was a particular favourite of Jill's when she sampled it on the show. The chicken-watermelon-spinach trio with the tang of feta cheese and a lemon vinaigrette is a winner.

VINAIGRETTE:

2–3 tbsp	**fresh lemon juice, to taste**	30–45 mL
½ tsp	**Dijon mustard**	2.5 mL
¼ cup	**olive oil**	60 mL
	salt and pepper to taste	

SALAD:

1	**single chicken breast (about 4 1/2 oz /112 g each), deboned, skinned, grilled or roasted**	1
4 cups	**watercress, baby spinach or arugula, or a combination**	1 L
2 cups	**watermelon, seeded, sliced into bite-size cubes**	500 mL

GARNISH:

½ cup	**feta cheese**	125 mL
½ cup	**pine nuts, toasted**	125 mL

METHOD:

In a small bowl, combine the lemon juice and mustard, then add the oil slowly. Add pepper and salt to taste. Can be made a day or two ahead of using. Refrigerate.

TO SERVE:

Cut the chicken on the diagonal into thin slices. In a salad bowl, combine the greens, watermelon and chicken slices. Toss with enough vinaigrette to just coat.

Divide among 4 salad plates. Sprinkle each plate with the feta cheese and pine nuts. Serve immediately.

GAYDA AND SARA'S CHINESE SALAD

Serves 8–10

This Oriental salad was served at meet director Ken Elmer and his wife Jan Neufeld's post-Achilles Harry Jerome International Track Classic volunteers' party, prepared for the buffet by one of the longtime volunteers, Gayda Coblin. Everyone raved about it. She kindly sent along the recipe to me, explaining that her friend Sara Ciacci had given it to her after receiving it from yet another friend.

So it is with recipes handed on from one person to another. As the great chef Julia Child commented: "There are no original recipes." Ingredients and methods are continually changed to make every recipe unique, and in that tradition this one will surely be passed on to many other friends!

SALAD:

1 head	**sui choy cabbage, finely sliced**	1 head
1 bunch	**green onions, finely sliced**	1 bunch
2 pkgs	**Ichiban noodles**	2 pkgs
½ cup	**sesame seeds, toasted**	125 mL
¾ cup	**slivered almonds, toasted**	175 mL
⅓ cup	**butter**	80 mL

DRESSING:

¾ cup	**vegetable oil**	175 mL
½ cup	**sugar**	125 mL
½ cup	**rice wine vinegar**	125 mL
2 tsp	**soy sauce**	10 mL

METHOD:

Crumble the noodles with your hands in the package before opening. Put in large bowl. Add the sesame seeds and the almonds.

In a large fry pan, melt the butter and sauté the crushed noodles, sesame seed and almonds until golden brown. Add the seasoning from the noodle packages, mix thoroughly. Drain the noodle mixture on paper towels for about an hour to remove the excess fat. Put back into salad bowl, add the onion and cabbage to the noodle mixture. Add the dressing, toss well and serve.

WHITE BEAN SALAD
WITH TUNA

Serves 6–8

This salad makes a tasty antipasto platter on its own. Have plenty of baguette bread on hand. I use canned white beans to get a jump-start on preparation. You can omit the tuna if you wish.

VINAIGRETTE:

2–3 tbsp	**red or white wine vinegar, to taste**	30–45 mL
½ tsp	**Dijon mustard**	2.5 mL
1	**clove garlic, pressed**	1
1 tbsp each	**fresh thyme and marjoram**	15 mL each
	OR	
1 tsp	**herbes de Provence**	5 mL
	salt and pepper to taste	
½ cup	**olive oil**	125 mL

SALAD:

28 oz	**can white cannellini beans, drained**	840 mL
½ cup	**red onions, finely chopped**	125 mL
2	**large tomatoes, seeded, coarsely chopped**	2
½	**red pepper, finely chopped**	½
½	**yellow pepper, finely chopped**	½
2 tbsp	**parsley, finely chopped**	30 mL
	salt and pepper to taste	
2	**7 oz / 184 g cans solid white tuna, packed in olive oil (optional)**	2
½ cup	**kalamata or green Mediterranean olives**	125 mL

METHOD:

In a small bowl whisk all the vinaigrette ingredients, adding the olive oil slowly at the end. Can be made a day or two ahead of serving. Refrigerate.

TO SERVE:

In a serving bowl, toss all the salad ingredients except the tuna and olives with enough of the dressing to just coat. Pile into a serving platter. Break the tuna into small pieces, arrange on top of the bean salad. Sprinkle the olives around the outside of the salad and serve. Can be made early in the day and left at room temperature, but add the tuna just before serving.

PRAWN AND CHERRY TOMATO SALAD

Serves 2–4 as a salad, 6–8 as an appetizer.

This versatile salad can also be served as an appetizer course. The jalapeno peppers give a little bite to it. Prepare the salad a few hours before serving and refrigerate.

SALAD:

1 lb	medium prawns, cooked, peeled (25–30)	450 g
10–12	cherry tomatoes, halved	10–12
3	jalapeno peppers, seeded, finely chopped	3
3 tbsp	fresh dill, chopped	45 mL
	salt and pepper to taste	

METHOD:

In a salad bowl, combine the prawns, tomatoes, chili peppers, fresh dill, salt and pepper. Add the salad dressing and toss lightly. Refrigerate.

DRESSING:

½ cup	mayonnaise	125 mL
2 tbsp	sherry vinegar or white wine vinegar	30 mL
	zest and juice of 2 large limes, or to taste	
2 tsp	grainy Dijon mustard	10 mL
	salt and pepper to taste	

METHOD:

In a small bowl, combine the dressing ingredients and blend well. Can be made a day ahead and refrigerated.

GARNISH:

Additional chopped fresh dill

TO SERVE:

As a salad for 2–4 people, add 2–3 cups seasonal greens. Place a few greens in the centre of each salad plate. Divide the prawn salad evenly in the middle of the greens. Sprinkle with additional chopped fresh dill and serve.

As an appetizer for 6–8, add 3–4 Belgian endive spears, separated. Mound the prawn salad on a serving platter, sprinkle with additional chopped fresh dill. Surround the salad on the outside with the Belgian endive spears and let your guests spoon some of the salad onto each spear.

SPINACH-GRAPEFRUIT SALAD

Serves 8

I always think of this as an après-ski or summertime barbecue salad. I particularly enjoy serving it as a starter course followed by the **French Canadian Tourtière with Sour Cream Sauce** (pg. 196) or **Gary's BBQ Salmon Fillet** (pg. 160).

SALAD:

3	10 oz/300 mL bags of spinach	3
5	hard-cooked eggs	5
6 slices	bacon, crisp-fried, cut into squares	6 slices
1 cup	fresh grapefruit slices, white or pink, or a combination	250 mL
½	red onion, thinly sliced	½
⅓ cup	toasted sesame seeds or sunflower seeds	80 mL

METHOD:

A day or two ahead of serving, wash the spinach greens, pat dry, put in plastic bag and refrigerate. The eggs, bacon and grapefruit can be prepared the morning of serving.

DRESSING:

1	egg	1
1 tsp	Dijon mustard	5 mL
1	clove garlic, crushed	1
2 tbsp	fresh grated Parmesan cheese	30 mL
	juice of 1 lemon	
1 tsp	sugar	5 mL
	dash of Worcestershire sauce	
½ cup	vegetable oil (or half vegetable oil, half olive oil)	125 mL

METHOD:

A day or two ahead of serving, combine all dressing ingredients, ending with slowly whisking in the oil to blend well. Refrigerate.

TO SERVE:

In a large bowl, tear the spinach into bite-size pieces. Pour over enough of the dressing to coat, and toss well. Peel the eggs, coarsely chop and add to the spinach, saving a few slices for garnish. Add the bacon and grapefruit and toss gently. Decorate top with the sliced eggs and onions. Add a sprinkling of toasted sesame or sunflower seeds for added crunch.

SUMMER
STRAWBERRY-SPINACH SALAD

Serves 6–8

The tart lemon dressing enhances the sweetness of summer's first strawberries. Although the dressing has egg yolks, you need only a little dressing per serving. Serve small portions as a starter course. Men love this salad!

SALAD:

2	10 oz / 250 g bags of baby spinach	2
1	basket fresh strawberries (3–4 per person), sliced	1
¾ cup	toasted sliced almonds	175 mL

METHOD:

A day or two ahead of serving, wash and pat dry the spinach greens. Put in plastic bag, refrigerate. Toast the almonds, put in container, refrigerate.

LEMON DRESSING:

½ cup	fine berry sugar	125 mL
2	large egg yolks	2
	juice of 2 lemons	
¾ cup	vegetable oil	175 mL

METHOD:

A day ahead of serving, make the dressing by combining sugar and lemon juice and stirring until sugar is dissolved. Add the egg yolks and whisk until creamy. Slowly whisk in the oil until thick and creamy. Refrigerate.

TO SERVE:

Divide the spinach among 6 salad plates, mounding in the centre. Scatter the strawberries over the spinach. Shake the dressing before pouring, drizzle a little of it over the spinach and strawberries. Sprinkle the almonds on top. Serve immediately.

TROPICAL SALAD

The perfect salad starter for a summer-evening barbecue, especially with grilled tuna or salmon.

SALAD:

1 cup	**fresh pineapple, cored, cut into chunks**	250 mL
1 cup	**fresh peeled or canned lychees, cut in half**	250 mL
1	**red apple, unpeeled, cut into cubes**	1
1	**large orange, peeled, cut into sections**	1
½ cup	**green or purple grapes**	125 mL
2	**large heads romaine lettuce**	2

METHOD:

A day or two ahead, wash and dry the lettuce, put in a plastic bag. Refrigerate.

DRESSING:

½ cup	**white wine vinegar or raspberry vinegar**	125 mL
¼ cup	**vegetable oil**	60 mL
1 tbsp	**lemon juice**	15 mL
1 tbsp	**fresh tarragon, finely chopped (optional)**	15 mL
3–4 tbsp	**honey**	45–60 mL

METHOD:

A day ahead, in a small bowl, whisk the dressing ingredients until blended thoroughly. Refrigerate.

TO SERVE:

On the day of serving, prepare the fruit. Toss the apple cubes with a little lemon or orange juice to prevent browning. If the grapes are large, cut them in half. Mix the fruit with a little of the dressing and refrigerate until ready to serve. Break the romaine lettuce into bite-size pieces; in a large salad bowl, toss the fruit gently with the romaine. Add enough dressing to coat. Serve immediately.

WILD RICE SALAD

Serves 6–8

The queen of rice, combined with hazelnuts and peppers with a ginger-chutney dressing, is one of my most requested recipes. Make this dish a day ahead to allow the flavours to mingle. It will keep for several days in the refrigerator.

SALAD:

1 cup	**wild rice**	250 mL
2 qt	**water**	1.9 L
½ cup	**toasted hazelnuts, coarsely chopped**	125 mL
⅓ cup	**green onions, finely chopped**	80 mL
½	**red pepper, finely chopped**	½
½	**yellow pepper, finely chopped**	½
½ cup	**golden raisins**	125 mL
	pinch of salt	

METHOD:

Wash rice well in strainer, rinsing with cold water for several minutes. Put rice in saucepan with the water, bring to a boil and simmer, uncovered, for 25–30 minutes until rice is tender. Don't overcook: the rice grains should be unpopped and still crunchy. Drain well and cool. Toss in a salad bowl with the remaining ingredients, with enough of the dressing to coat well. Cover and refrigerate.

TO SERVE:

Just before serving, toss with more of the dressing. If you like lots of crunch, don't add the nuts until the very last minute. For variety, use pistachios instead of hazelnuts.

GINGER-CHUTNEY DRESSING:

1 cup	vegetable oil	250 mL
2 tbsp	rice wine vinegar	30 mL
3 tbsp	Major Grey's Mango Chutney or other fruit chutney	45 mL
2 tbsp	Chinese candied ginger in syrup, finely chopped	30 mL
2 tbsp	candied ginger syrup pepper to taste	30 mL
2 tbsp	soy sauce	30 mL
2 tbsp	honey	30 mL

METHOD:

Blend dressing ingredients well. Can be made several days ahead and refrigerated.

DIANE'S SECRETS:

Try the Ginger-Chutney Dressing tossed with seasonal greens, sesame seeds and slices of orange and mango.

TRIO OF
POTATO SALADS

Over the years, I've made tons of potato salad. These three are my all-time best, each with a personality all its own!

HOT POTATO SALAD

Serves 10–12

This warm potato salad goes well with any barbecue menu and can also be served cold. Basil is the teaser herb in this salad!

SALAD:

8 cups	tiny new red potatoes, cooked and cubed	2 L
1 cup	fresh corn kernels, cooked (can use frozen)	250 mL
½ cup	red pepper, finely chopped	125 mL
½ cup	yellow pepper, finely chopped	125 mL
3	medium tomatoes, peeled, seeded, cubed	3
	salt and pepper to taste	

METHOD:

A day ahead of serving, combine all the ingredients; add enough of the following dressing to coat well. Cover and refrigerate. Next morning you will need to add more dressing to the potatoes, as they absorb some overnight. To serve warm, simply heat everything in a heavy skillet.

DRESSING:

1 cup	fresh basil leaves, finely chopped	250 mL
¼ cup	olive or vegetable oil, or a combination	60 mL
1 tsp	Dijon mustard	5 mL
4 tbsp	red wine vinegar	60 mL
5 tbsp	green onions or shallots, finely chopped	75 mL
	salt and pepper to taste	

METHOD:

Combine all ingredients in a food processor, adding the oil slowly. Can be made a day ahead of serving. Refrigerate.

PESTO POTATO SALAD

Serves 8–12

When tiny summer potatoes and green beans are at their sweetest, cook them gently and toss with your favourite homemade or deli pesto. Make the salad a day or two ahead for best flavour and serve hot or cold.

8 cups	**baby new potatoes, red or white, or a combination**	2 L
3 cups	**fresh green beans, sliced diagonally**	750 mL
½ cup	**radishes, thinly sliced**	125 mL
1	**small red onion, finely chopped, about 1 cup / 250 mL**	1
	salt, pepper to taste	
½ cup	**pesto, or to taste**	125 mL
½ cup	**grated Parmesan cheese**	125 mL

METHOD:

Cut potatoes into halves or quarters, cover with cold water and boil gently until they are just tender, 10–15 minutes. Blanch the beans for about 3 minutes, until slightly crunchy: don't overcook. Drain and cool the vegetables.

TO SERVE:

In a large salad bowl, toss the potatoes, beans, radishes and chopped onion. Add salt and pepper to taste and toss again with the pesto to coat well. Cover and refrigerate.

To serve hot, put into a large skillet and stir over medium heat until just heated through. Sprinkle a little of the Parmesan cheese on each serving.

DIANE'S SECRETS:

Purchase your pesto from a deli or specialty grocery if you don't have time to make your own — and who has?

CREAMY POTATO DILL SALAD

Serves 8–12

"Like no other" is the response I get whenever I have served this salad over the years! Many people can relate it to their childhood and summer picnics with Mom's own special potato salad. "What exactly do you put in your salad"? I'm asked. My secret is this: It's the addition of grainy Dijon mustard and a little sour cream that makes the difference. "Ahhh, that's what it is!" they exclaim. Those secret ingredients came from my mom's Maritime potato salad.

8 cups	cooked baby new potatoes, red or white	2 L
1 cup	red onion, finely chopped	250 mL
2 cups	mayonnaise	500 mL
½ cup	sour cream	125 mL
⅓ cup	grainy Dijon mustard, or to taste	80 mL
	lots of cracked pepper, salt to taste	
½ cup	fresh dill, chopped	125 mL

METHOD:

A day ahead or on the morning of serving, cut the potatoes into halves or quarters. Add the rest of the ingredients to make a super-creamy combination. The potatoes will absorb a lot of the mayonnaise and sour cream, so you might need to add a little more of each if you find it is not creamy enough.

DIANE'S SECRETS:

Start with less of the grainy Dijon mustard than I've suggested, then add more to taste. I like lots of mustard, but you may like it tamer.

RED CABBAGE SALAD
WITH FETA CHEESE

Serves 6–8

The combination of cabbage, feta cheese and toasted pecans is enhanced with a tangy lemon-mustard dressing. Great with grilled or baked fish.

SALAD:

4 cups	**red cabbage, cored, thinly shredded**	1 L
¾ cup	**toasted pecan halves**	175 mL
½–¾ cup	**feta cheese, cubed**	125–175 mL
3	**Granny Smith apples, cored, coarsely chopped**	3

DRESSING:

	zest and juice of 1 large lemon	
2 tbsp	**red wine vinegar**	30 mL
1 tsp	**Dijon mustard**	5 mL
2 tbsp	**honey**	30 mL
	salt and pepper to taste	
½ cup	**vegetable oil**	125 mL

METHOD:

A day or two ahead of serving, in a small bowl whisk the dressing ingredients, slowly adding the vegetable oil. Refrigerate.

TO SERVE:

A few hours before serving, shred the cabbage. Toss with the dressing to coat well. Check seasonings. Just before serving, add the pecans, feta and apples. Toss well and serve.

GRILLED TUNA SALAD

Serves 4

During our stay in Maui we had fresh sashimi tuna at least three times a week. The simple preparation and combination of Asian ingredients put this salad at the top of our list! Serve with a basket of crispy wontons (see **New York Duck Salad**, pg. 104) or a sourdough baguette. The Soy-Ginger Vinaigrette here is equally tasty added to the greens for the **Maui Prawns** (pg.31)

TUNA RUB:

8 oz	**sashimi-grade tuna**	200 g
2 tbsp	**freshly ground pepper**	30 mL
2 tbsp	**peeled fresh ginger, very finely chopped**	30 mL
	peanut oil	

METHOD:

Just before serving, on a dinner plate combine the pepper and ginger. Coat the tuna all over with this mixture. Heat a little of the peanut oil in a grill pan or barbecue, grill the tuna for about 2 minutes per side, more if you like it not so rare. Don't overcook. Set aside while you toss the greens.

SALAD AND GARNISH:

4 cups	**mixed greens**	1 L
	Soy-Ginger Vinaigrette	
	toasted sesame seeds, white and black	

GARNISH:

½ cup	**carrot, finely grated**	125 mL
½ cup	**daikon radish, finely grated**	125 mL
4	**lime wedges**	4

--- D A I K O N ---

Daikon is a large, tapered white radish with a slightly hot flavour, usually grated and served as a garnish or condiment with Asian food.

SOY-GINGER VINAIGRETTE:

2 tbsp	soy sauce	30 mL
	juice of 1/4 lime	
1 tbsp	shallots, finely chopped	15 mL
1	clove garlic, pressed	1
2 tbsp	Chinese sweet chili sauce	30 mL
	pepper to taste	
1 tbsp	pure sesame oil	15 mL
½ cup	peanut oil	125 mL

METHOD:

In a small bowl, whisk all the vinaigrette ingredients, adding the sesame and peanut oils very slowly. Can be made a day or two ahead of serving. Refrigerate.

TO SERVE:

In a salad bowl, toss the mixed greens with just enough Soy-Ginger Vinaigrette to coat. Mound equal amounts on 4 salad plates. Slice the tuna thinly and divide evenly, fan-shape, on top of the greens. Sprinkle with a few sesame seeds. Arrange small mounds of the carrot and daikon garnish on the plate. Add a lime wedge. Pass more dressing if desired.

DIANE'S SECRETS:

The toasted sesame seeds, white and black, can be found at specialty Asian stores. To toast your own sesame seeds, spread them on a cookie sheet and roast in a 350°F/180°C oven for about 5 minutes. Watch carefully, or they will burn and taste bitter.

ORIENTAL NOODLE SALAD

Serves 6–8

This recipe is one of my classics. It's a meal in itself, or will add to any summertime buffet. It's best made a day ahead and is a perfect picnic salad.

SALAD:

2	**12 oz / 300 g package steam-fried or dry Chinese egg noodles for chow mein**	2
2 tbsp	**pure sesame oil**	30 mL
¾ cup	**water chestnuts, finely chopped**	175 mL
½ cup	**green onions, finely chopped**	125 mL
½ cup	**red and yellow peppers, finely chopped**	125 mL
1 cup	**carrots, finely chopped and lightly blanched**	250 mL
3 tbsp	**toasted sesame seeds**	45 mL
½ cup	**cashew nuts, coarsely chopped**	125 mL

METHOD:

Boil the noodles according to directions; drain. Rinse well and toss with the sesame oil. Mix with rest of ingredients, adding enough dressing to coat all ingredients well. Cover and refrigerate overnight. Before serving, you may have to add a little more dressing if it seems too dry.

DIANE'S SECRETS:

Deep, mellow and salty-sweet, tamari sauce is brewed from soybeans, water and salt and contains no wheat. This gives it a different flavour from soy sauce.

DRESSING:

½ cup	**creamy or chunky peanut butter**	125 mL
¼ cup	**Chinese tamari sauce**	60 mL
¼ cup	**soy sauce**	60 mL
3	**cloves garlic, pressed**	3
2 tbsp	**pure sesame oil**	30 mL
4 tbsp	**rice wine vinegar or sherry**	60 mL
¼ cup	**red pepper oil**	60 mL

(can be purchased in a Chinese food section, or make your own)

METHOD:

In a food processor, blend all the ingredients until smooth. Can be made 2–3 days ahead of serving. Refrigerate. Any leftover dressing can be used as a sauce or dip for fish and meats.

RED PEPPER OIL:

In a small saucepan, add ½ tsp / 2.5 mL red pepper flakes to 2 tbsp / 30 mL oil, bring to a boil and let sit for about 10 minutes. Strain. Will keep for several days. If you want a more intense flavour, let it sit for 15–20 minutes longer.

NEW YORK DUCK SALAD
WITH CRISPY WONTONS

Serves 8–10

I have often demonstrated this salad on television and at cooking schools. It's always a hit! The tart lime dressing and the barbecued duck are a perfect balance for the mixed greens and fried wontons. Barbecued duck can be purchased at most Chinese delis or meat markets. If you can't find it, try the recipe with fresh shrimp, chicken or pork instead. Makes a unique salad course or light summer dinner.

SALAD:

2	whole barbecued duck, skinned, boned, sliced in thin strips (about 2 cups /500 mL) or substitute shrimp, chicken or pork	2
10–12 cups	mixed greens	2.5–3 L
¼ cup	toasted sesame seeds	60 mL
¾ cup	sliced toasted almonds	175 mL

DRESSING:

3	slices peeled ginger, finely chopped (about 2 tbsp /30 mL)	3
	zest of 3 limes, finely chopped	
½ cup	lime juice	125 mL
2–3 tbsp	brown sugar	30–45 mL
3	cloves garlic, finely chopped	3
2–3 tbsp	Chinese sweet chili sauce	30–45 mL
⅓ cup	shallots or green onions, finely chopped	80 mL
	salt and pepper to taste	
¾ cup	vegetable oil	175 mL

METHOD:

In a medium bowl, whisk all the dressing ingredients until well blended, slowly adding the vegetable oil. Refrigerate. Can be made 2–3 days ahead of serving.

CRISPY WONTONS:

1 lb	package whole egg wonton skins	450 g
	peanut oil	

METHOD:

On the day of serving, cut the wonton skins into thin ¼-inch/.5-cm strips. Cover the base of a large skillet with about 2 in/5 cm of peanut oil and heat; the oil is hot enough when a strip of wonton skin begins to curl. Add a few strips at a time and fry for only a few seconds, until they turn golden. (Watch that they don't get too brown: If they overbrown they will be bitter, so discard and start again. Adjust the heat if the oil is too hot.) Remove with a strainer spoon, drain well on paper towels. Put in a serving basket and set aside. Can be made on the morning of serving and left at room temperature.

TO SERVE:

Toss the greens with enough dressing to coat lightly, then arrange on salad plates for individual servings, or on a large, shallow platter. Cover with a layer of the duck, then almonds, then sesame seeds and, finally, a few crispy wontons. Serve the remaining wontons in a basket. Pass more dressing.

BLUE CHEESE
WALNUT SALAD

Serves 6

Doug and I had this tangy salad at Café Une, Deux, Trois restaurant in the theatre district in New York many years ago. I don't know if the restaurant still exists, but I do know this salad is super! It's important to use a good quality French blue cheese that crumbles easily, and fresh walnuts. The blue cheese flavour is very mild, so even those who shy away from pungent cheeses will actually enjoy it. Use Spartan or Granny Smith apples.

SALAD:

2–3	**heads of romaine lettuce**	2–3
¼ cup	**French blue cheese, crumbled**	60 mL
½ cup	**fresh roasted walnuts, halved or in large pieces**	125 mL
2	**medium apples, cored and cubed**	2

METHOD:

A day or two ahead, wash and dry the romaine, put in plastic bag. Refrigerate. Roast the walnuts.

DRESSING:

¼ cup	**sherry wine vinegar**	60 mL
	salt and pepper to taste	
½ cup	**olive oil**	125 mL

METHOD:

In a small combine, whisk the dressing ingredients, adding the oil slowly. Can be made a day or so ahead. Refrigerate.

TO SERVE:

Break the romaine into bite-size pieces. Put into a large salad bowl. In a separate bowl, toss together the cheese, walnuts and apples with a bit of the dressing, spoon into the centre of the salad bowl. Drizzle over just enough dressing to coat the greens, sprinkle with pepper. Toss and serve.

SALAD DRESSINGS

It's so easy to whip up an endless variety of dressings, and once you start making your own you will rarely pick one off a grocery shelf, though I must confess that now and then I buy a dressing or two from one of my favourite gourmet delis when I'm strapped for time.

These are a few of my classic salad dressings; from the basic balsamic to citrus ginger, every taste bud is satisfied! The secret of an outstanding salad dressing is to use superior quality oils and vinegars. Add the oils as the last ingredient, very slowly. I usually make my dressings at least two days before serving, to allow the flavours to develop. Shake well before using.

BALSAMIC VINAIGRETTE

1 cup	**olive oil, or a blend of vegetable and olive oil**	250 mL	**METHOD:**
4–5 tbsp	**balsamic vinegar, or to taste**	60–75 mL	Whisk together until well blended. Add more vinegar and mustard if desired.
1 tsp	**Dijon mustard**	5 mL	
	salt and pepper to taste		

VARIATIONS:

"FROM THE GARDEN" BALSAMIC VINAIGRETTE: To the basic Balsamic Vinaigrette recipe add 3–4 tbsp/45–60 mL chopped green onions or shallots, 3 tbsp/45 mL fresh grated Parmesan cheese and 1 tbsp/15 mL fresh herbs, such as basil, oregano or dill.

SUN-DRIED TOMATO OR OLIVE VINAIGRETTE: To the basic Balsamic Vinaigrette recipe add 3 tbsp/45 mL of sun-dried tomato pesto or olive tapenade and whisk well. Try it over a tomato, onion, bocconcini salad with fresh basil — DYNAMITE!

MAPLE BALSAMIC VINAIGRETTE: Add 3–4 tbsp /45–60 mL pure maple syrup to the basic Balsamic Vinaigrette recipe. Taste for the balance of sweet / sour between the vinegar and the maple syrup.

WESTCOASTER SALAD: This maple vinaigrette is ideal to show off our West Coast peppered salmon. My favourite is Westcoast Select (Sundance). In a saucepan, over low heat, warm some of the dressing. Add a few julienned slices of red and yellow peppers and several thin slices of the peppered salmon. Warm slightly over low heat.

TO SERVE:

For each serving, mound some seasonal greens on a salad plate. Drizzle over a little of the dressing mixture. Top with a few pieces of chèvre and serve immediately.

YOGURT-DILL DRESSING

Refreshing, tangy and low in fat! How can you lose?

1 ⅓ cup	low-fat plain yogurt	325 mL	METHOD:
1 ½ tbsp	white wine vinegar	20 mL	Whisk all in a bowl to blend well. Refrigerate for up
1 ½ tbsp	fresh lemon juice	20 mL	to one week.
½ tbsp	Worcestershire sauce	10 mL	
½ tbsp	Dijon mustard	10 mL	
2	cloves garlic, crushed	2	
½ cup	fresh dill, chopped	125 mL	
1 cup	olive oil	250 mL	

ORANGE MUSTARD DRESSING

A taste of the Orient with a hint of ginger, sesame oil and rice wine vinegar. Very light, very delightful! To serve this dressing with mixed greens, add enough just to coat the greens, then decorate with orange slices, thin red onion rings, thin slices of red and yellow peppers and a sprinkle of toasted sesame seeds. This is one of my all-time most-requested dressings.

1 ½ cups	orange juice concentrate, undiluted	375 mL	**METHOD:**
¼ cup	rice wine vinegar	60 mL	Whisk well to blend. Refrigerate for up to 4–5 days.
2 tbsp	Dijon mustard	30 mL	
1 cup	olive oil	250 mL	
3 tbsp	fresh peeled ginger, finely minced	45 mL	
¼ cup	pure sesame oil	60 mL	
	pinch of crushed red chili pepper flakes		
1 tbsp	lemon juice	15 mL	

LEMON MASCARPONE DRESSING

Try this delicate lemon dressing drizzled over perfectly ripened avocado slices and orange slices on a bed of Belgian endive sliced in thin strips. Very sensuous! Also interesting drizzled on **Roasted Asparagus Bocconcini Salad** (pg. 82).

1 tbsp	**lemon zest, finely chopped**	15 mL	METHOD:
¼ cup	**lemon juice**	60 mL	In a food processor, blend all the ingredients,
¼ cup	**Italian mascarpone cheese**	60 mL	slowly adding the olive oil until creamy.
1 cup	**olive oil**	250 mL	Refrigerate for up to 3 days.
	salt and pepper to taste		

Vegetab

les

ORIENTAL FRIED VEGETABLE RICE

Serves 12

On one of our visits to New York we dined at The China Grill, where a cross-cultural style of cooking reigns supreme. The results are always superb. This fried rice creation and their Duck Salad were voted the most popular dishes among our party that evening. This is an adaptation of the rice dish. The rice can be cooked and the vegetables chopped the day ahead. The dish can be finished on the morning of serving, kept covered in a skillet or a wok, then quickly reheated just before guests arrive. It goes well with any grilled meats, seafood or poultry.

6 cups	cooked brown rice	1.5 L
3 tbsp	vegetable oil	45 mL
1 cup	carrots	250 mL
1 cup	broccoli	250 mL
½ cup	shallots	125 mL
1	red pepper	1
1	yellow pepper	1
1 cup	green onions, chopped	250 mL
1 cup	asparagus, sliced diagonally	250 mL
1 tbsp	fresh ginger, finely chopped	15 mL
2	cloves garlic, finely chopped	2
¼ tsp	red pepper flakes	1 mL
1	large egg, slightly beaten (optional)	1
	pepper to taste	
¼ cup	soy sauce	60 mL

METHOD:

Cut the asparagus on the diagonal into small thin slices and dice the rest of the vegetables finely: they must be in very small cubes to cook quickly. Heat a large wok or skillet for about 20 seconds on high heat, then add the oil. Add the carrots, sauté for about 2 minutes, then add the rest of the vegetables and the ginger, garlic and red pepper flakes. Stir-fry for about 2 minutes and don't overcook: the vegetables should be slightly crunchy. Add the beaten egg and stir. Add cooked rice and continue to stir mixture in the wok for about 3 minutes (if using a skillet, shake the pan frequently). Add pepper and soy sauce and continue to cook for a minute or two. Transfer to a large platter or casserole and serve immediately, or refrigerate overnight. Just before serving, reheat in a 350°F/180°C oven for 35–40 minutes or until hot. Any leftovers can be frozen.

THAI RICE WITH COCONUT MILK

Usually found in Oriental markets, Thai rice is slightly sticky when cooked. The canned coconut milk will give it a creamy, subtle flavour. For garnish I use black sesame seeds, but plain sesame seeds toasted to a golden brown will do as well. Goes well with any Oriental fish and meat dishes. The sesame seasoning teases your palate as you bite into the rice square. Try Thai black rice for a change.

2 cups	**raw Thai rice**	500 mL
2 cups	**water**	500 mL
2 cups	**canned coconut milk**	500 mL
	sesame seeds, black or toasted	

METHOD:

In a saucepan, bring water and coconut milk to a boil. Add the rice, stir. Cover the pot and simmer for about 20 minutes, or until the liquid has been absorbed. Stir well to blend.

TO SERVE: Shape the rice into squares — being slightly sticky, it moulds easily. Top each square with sesame seeds. Or fluff the rice with a fork and sprinkle with a little sesame seasoning.

SESAME POWDER SEASONING:

¼ cup	**white sesame seeds**	60 mL
1 tsp	**sea salt**	5 mL

METHOD:

Heat a small, heavy skillet. Add the sesame seeds and the salt, stir for about 4 minutes, or until the sesame seeds are golden. Stir constantly so that they won't burn; otherwise, the seeds become bitter and you'll have to start again. Cool and grind seeds to a powder.

DIANE'S SECRETS:

The Sesame Powder Seasoning will keep for weeks in a covered jar, and is a tasty addition sprinkled over any Asian dish.

ORZO WITH PARMESAN CHEESE

Serves 8

Orzo is a rice-shaped pasta that can usually be obtained from Italian or specialty markets. It's a perfect accompaniment to the **Tuscan Chicken** (pg. 176), or any other Italian meat or fish dish. Have a bowl of Parmesan cheese to pass for those who love their Parmesan!

2 cups	**raw orzo**	500 mL
4–6 tbsp	**butter**	60–90 mL
4–6 tbsp	**chicken or vegetable stock**	60–90 mL
6–8 tbsp	**Parmesan cheese, freshly grated**	90–120 mL
	salt and pepper to taste	
4–5 tbsp	**parsley, finely chopped**	60–75 mL

METHOD:

A day ahead or on the morning of serving, cook the orzo in a large Dutch oven with plenty of salted water for 10–12 minutes or until barely tender and doubled in volume. Do not overcook. Drain well in a colander, rinsing with plenty of cold water to remove excess starch. Drain again.

Melt the butter in a large, heavy fry pan; add the orzo and heat through. Add just enough stock to moisten the orzo; stir in the Parmesan cheese. Add the salt and pepper to taste. Toss with chopped parsley and serve, or refrigerate overnight and reheat in a 350°F/180°C oven for 35–40 minutes or until hot.

DIANE'S SECRETS:

If made a day ahead, you might want to add a little more chicken stock and Parmesan cheese to moisten the orzo before reheating. Try adding sautéed mushrooms, prosciutto and roasted peppers for a whole meal in itself.

COUSCOUS WITH CHICK PEAS

Serves 10–12

Couscous is a cereal made from coarsely ground durum wheat (semolina). Use the instant variety; it works very well. This dish can be made ahead and reheated in a 350°F/180°C oven for 35–40 minutes, or until hot.

3 cups	**instant couscous**	750 mL
3 ¼ cups	**chicken stock**	810 mL
½ cup	**currants or raisins**	125 mL
15 oz	**can chick peas, drained**	375 g
½ tsp	**cinnamon**	2.5 mL
	pinch of saffron or turmeric	
	for colour and flavour (optional)	
	salt and pepper to taste	
2–3 tbsp	**chopped parsley**	30–45 mL

METHOD:

Bring the chicken stock to a boil. In a large saucepan, combine the stock with couscous, raisins, chick peas, spices and seasonings. Cover and let stand for about 5 minutes, or until all the liquid has been absorbed. Add parsley just before serving. Serve immediately, or cool and refrigerate, reheating when ready to serve. You might want to add a little more chicken stock to moisten the couscous if it seems a bit dry before serving.

TURMERIC

Turmeric comes in powdered form and is actually a root, a member of the ginger family. It contains a bright yellow dye that gives its distinctive colour to curries and other Asian and Far Eastern dishes. It can also be used in place of saffron to give colour to food, although it has a slightly bitter taste. Use sparingly.

BULGUR RICE PILAF

Serves 4–6

Chatelaine magazine featured this recipe in one of its issues and said, "It's the best bulgur wheat dish we've tested!" The combination of cracked bulgur wheat and brown rice spiked with turmeric and lemon gives my dish a unique flavour and nutlike texture. This recipe can be prepared a day ahead and reheated just before serving.

2 tbsp	butter	30 mL	
½ cup	onion, finely chopped	125 mL	
½ cup	uncooked bulgur wheat	125 mL	
½ cup	brown rice, washed and strained	125 mL	
½ tsp	turmeric	2.5 mL	
⅓ cup	currants or raisins (optional)	80 mL	
	salt and pepper to taste		
2 cups	chicken stock, heated to boiling	500 mL	
2 tbsp	parsley, chopped	30 mL	
	zest and juice of 1/2 lemon		
⅓ cup	toasted pecans, finely chopped (optional)	80 mL	

METHOD:

Melt the butter in a large saucepan. Add onion, bulgur, brown rice and turmeric and sauté until golden, about 4 minutes. Add rest of ingredients except parsley, lemon zest, lemon juice and pecans. Simmer for 30–35 minutes, covered, until all the liquid is absorbed. Add the remaining ingredients; toss and serve. If preparing ahead, refrigerate after simmering. To reheat, bake in a 350°F/180°C oven for 25–30 minutes, or until hot.

NOTE: 2 ½ cups/625 mL of uncooked brown rice will yield 6 cups/1.5 L cooked. Rinse uncooked rice and add to 4 cups/1 L water. Bring to a boil and simmer for 45–50 minutes or until all the liquid is absorbed. Keep checking after 40 minutes to make sure you don't burn the rice on the bottom.

RISOTTO VARIATIONS

BASIC ITALIAN RISOTTO

Serves 6 as a main course

Risotto makes a fabulous meal on its own, served with an antipasto platter, hearty bread and Italian wines. Our family never tires of this classic Italian dish, using the special stubby grain rice known as "arborio" that gives the risotto its distinct creamy texture. You have to be patient when preparing this dish, as it takes constant stirring for about 25 minutes for a perfect risotto, but it's worth it! I usually prepare the first stage earlier on the day of serving and do the final stage just before serving.

The variations to the classic risotto are endless. Some of my favourite additions to the basic risotto recipe are chicken or seafood, roasted wild mushrooms or butternut squash.

2–3 tbsp	butter	30–45 mL
½ cup	onions, finely chopped	125 mL
¼ cup	shallots, finely chopped	60 mL
2	cloves garlic, pressed	2
2 cups	raw arborio rice	500 mL
1 cup	dry white wine	250 mL
7–8 cups	chicken stock, heated	1.75–2 L
	salt and pepper to taste	
	about 1 1/2 cups / 375 mL	
	Parmesan cheese, freshly grated	

METHOD:

A few hours before serving, melt the butter in a heavy saucepan over moderate heat and add the onions, shallots and garlic. Sauté for a few minutes until golden and translucent. Add the rice, stir for a few more minutes (you can prepare the rice to this stage earlier on the day of serving). Set aside until ready to commence this final preparation: Add the white wine, stir until absorbed. Begin adding one ladle of the hot chicken stock at a time, every few minutes, stirring all the while and keeping the rice at a constant simmer. Cook for about 25 minutes, or until the rice is *al dente* and the risotto is creamy. Add ½ cup/125 mL of the Parmesan cheese to the rice for the last 5 minutes of cooking; add salt and pepper to taste. Add more stock if you think the risotto is too dry. Have the extra Parmesan cheese in a bowl for your guests to sprinkle on top of the rice.

CHICKEN RISOTTO:

To the basic risotto recipe, add 2 cooked chicken breasts, sliced or cubed, at the same time that you add the last ladle of chicken stock. Stir gently, adding the Parmesan cheese to the rice to finish the risotto.

SEAFOOD RISOTTO:

To the basic risotto recipe, add ½ pound / 225 g each of raw, peeled, medium prawns, halved scallops and cubed salmon as you add the last ladle of chicken stock. Stir gently for about 5 minutes, or until the seafood is opaque. Add the Parmesan cheese to the rice to finish the risotto.

Some Italian chefs feel you shouldn't add Parmesan cheese to a seafood risotto, but it's up to you. I always add it, because I happen to love Parmesan!

ROASTED WILD MUSHROOM RISOTTO:

1	medium portobello mushroom, sliced	1	
½ cup	shiitake mushrooms, sliced	125 mL	
½ cup	chanterelle mushrooms (or any other variety), sliced	125 mL	
	salt and pepper to taste		
2 tbsp	olive oil	30 mL	

METHOD:

While the basic risotto is cooking, in a bowl toss the mushrooms with the olive oil, sprinkle with salt and pepper to taste. Put on a cookie sheet and roast in a 400°F/200°C oven for 10–12 minutes, or until softened. Add the mushrooms to the rice at the same time that you add the last ladle of chicken stock. Stir gently, add the Parmesan cheese, finish the risotto.

One cup/250 mL of blanched asparagus (about 6 spears), sliced on the diagonal, can be added to this risotto in the last five minutes if desired.

BUTTERNUT SQUASH RISOTTO:

3 lb	**butternut squash,**	1.35 kg
	peeled, seeded	
1	**6 1/2 oz/162.5 g roll of chèvre**	1

METHOD:

Bring 7–8 cups /1.75–2 L of chicken stock to a boil.
Julienne 1 cup /250 mL of squash; cube the rest.
Add the cubed squash to boiling stock and cook
15–20 minutes, or until the squash is soft. Purée
and set aside. Prepare the basic risotto recipe,
using the butternut squash purée stock. In the last
10 minutes of cooking, add the julienned strips of
squash and the Parmesan cheese to finish the
risotto. Serve with a wedge of chèvre on top of each
serving.

DIANE'S SECRETS:

Any leftover risotto can be reheated as
a pancake the next day. Moisten a
non-stick fry pan with a little oil, add
the risotto, pat down well as if you
were making hash brown potatoes.
Cook over medium heat for 6–8
minutes or until the rice is hot and
slightly golden. Flip over to brown the
other side. Serve in wedges, sprinkle
with a little extra Parmesan cheese.
Great with scrambled eggs for brunch!

POLENTA

Serves 6

Try polenta in place of pasta, potatoes or rice as a starch accompaniment to any meal. Don't be intimidated about making polenta: once you make it a few times, it becomes easy! Don't bother trying the "instant" variety; it's tasteless and the texture is like rubber.

7 cups	**water**	1.75 L
1 tbsp	**salt**	15 mL
1 tbsp	**olive oil**	15 mL
1 ⅔ cups	**yellow cornmeal, coarsely ground**	400 mL
2 tbsp	**butter**	30 mL
⅓ cup	**Parmesan cheese (optional)**	80 mL

METHOD:

In a large, heavy saucepan, combine the water, salt and olive oil and whisk in the cornmeal. Put the heat to medium-high and stir mixture constantly with a wooden spoon for about 5 minutes, or until the polenta boils and is slightly thickened. Reduce the heat to medium-low. Cook, stirring often for 30–35 minutes or until the polenta pulls away slightly from the bottom and sides of the saucepan. Add the butter and the Parmesan cheese, stir until blended.

TO SERVE:

You can serve the polenta while it's soft and creamy, or put it into an oiled casserole or pan until it is cooled. Then turn out, cut it into squares or wedges and grill until golden and crisp on the barbecue, or in a grill pan on top of the stove.

POTATOES GRATIN

Serves 8–10

Potatoes Gratin are one of the all-time comfort foods! I enjoy my Potatoes Gratin as a vegetable accompaniment to roasted chicken and meats. It can be baked ahead of time and reheated while the chicken or meat is roasting, which is ideal when entertaining.

2 tbsp	olive oil	30 mL
1 cup	shallots or onions, finely sliced	250 mL
2	cloves garlic, pressed	2
5	large baking potatoes, very thinly sliced	5
1 cup	half-and-half cream	250 mL
1 cup	whipping cream	250 mL
½ lb	Gruyère or Emmenthal cheese, or a combination, grated	225 g
	salt and pepper to taste	
½ cup	Parmesan cheese	125 mL

METHOD:

Butter a large gratin casserole, about 12 × 8½ × 2 in / 30 × 21 × 5 cm. Heat the olive oil in a skillet, add the shallots or onions, add garlic and sauté for about 3 minutes, or until softened. Set aside.

Peel and wash the potatoes. Slice thinly, put in a large bowl with the onion-garlic mixture. In a separate bowl, mix the half-and-half, whipping cream, cheese, salt and pepper. Add to the potatoes and mix well. Pour into the gratin casserole, pressing the potatoes down to coat well. Sprinkle the Parmesan cheese on top. Bake at 350°F/180°C for about 1 ½ hours, or until the top is golden and the potatoes cooked. Can be cooled, refrigerated a day ahead, then reheated in a 350°F/180°C oven for about 30 minutes or until hot.

DIANE'S SECRETS:

Substitute 2 cups/500 mL of chicken stock or skim milk for the half-and-half and cream for a gratin that is lower in fat content, but still delicious! You can also substitute 1 large fennel bulb, julienned, for the shallots or onions.

For thin potato slices, using a mandolin is the easiest and quickest way to go!

OVEN
FRENCH FRIES

Serves 6

These are quick to make, and healthy! The potatoes can be washed, peeled and sliced in cubes or strips ahead of time and kept in ice water; pat dry and bake just before serving. Great for dipping with **Quick Lemon Dill Mayonnaise** or **Quick Aioli Dip** (pg. 63).

6	**medium potatoes**	6
	vegetable oil	
½–¾ cup	**Parmesan cheese**, 125–175 mL	
	finely grated	
	salt to taste	

METHOD:

Preheat the oven to 425°F/210°C.

Peel the potatoes and cut into French fry slices (the length of the potato). Keep in ice water.

Just before serving, drain the potatoes and pat dry. Roll them in a little oil to coat and toss in the Parmesan cheese. Lightly oil a cookie sheet; place a lightly oiled long cake rake on the sheet. Spread the potatoes on top of the cake rack. Bake for about 55 minutes, tossing from time to time. For the last 10 minutes, remove the cake rack and spread the fries on the cookie sheet to crisp. When crispy and golden, they are ready to eat. Sprinkle with salt and serve immediately — watch them disappear!

RUTH'S **BAKED SPANISH** ONIONS

Serves 6–8

In the fall of 2001 my sister-in-law Ruth and brother Joel entertained Doug and me, my twin brother David and his wife Dianne at Ruth and Joel's home in Bedford Basin, Nova Scotia. In celebration of David's and my birthday we had a weekend of great wines, Nova Scotia lobster, grilled steaks, fresh seafood casserole and plenty of laughs! Ruth's Baked Spanish Onions were a big hit when she topped Joel's juicy slices of beef with the roasted onion slices. Try them next time you are in the mood for a good steak.

2	**large Spanish onions**	2
	olive or vegetable oil	

TOPPING:

¼ cup	**butter**	60 mL
½ cup	**fine dry bread crumbs**	125 mL
½ cup	**grated Swiss cheese**	125 mL
	or Parmesan cheese	
½ cup	**parsley, finely chopped**	125 mL
3	**cloves garlic, pressed**	3
	salt and pepper to taste	

METHOD:

Peel the onions, slice into 1-in/2.5-cm thick slices. Rub each with a little oil and place in a buttered (9 × 12 in/22.5 × 30 cm) casserole. Cover with tinfoil and bake in a 350°F/180°C oven for about 40 minutes, until softened. Remove pan from oven. Increase the oven heat to 450°F/230°C. Drain any liquid from the onion pan, put liquid in a small bowl. Combine the rest of the ingredients, add to the onion liquid, toss. Pour the topping mixture onto the cut surfaces of the onion. Bake for 5–7 minutes more, or until the topping is golden. Serve with grilled meat or fish.

ROASTED VEGETABLES

Roasting is such an easy way to prepare vegetables. Roasted veggies are part of our family's traditional turkey dinner, except for the potatoes: Those definitely have to be mashed to handle all that gravy! When roasting, allow one piece of each vegetable per person.

A combination of these or other vegetables (use your imagination!):

new baby potatoes

sweet potatoes

parsnips

turnips

beets

carrots

fennel

shallots

garlic cloves

olive oil

fresh rosemary sprigs, finely chopped, or herbes de Provence

METHOD:

Peel all vegetables except the new potatoes. Vary the shapes: for example, use 1-in/2.5-cm cubes of sweet potatoes, julienned strips of parsnips and turnips, quartered beets and so on.

In a large bowl, combine the olive oil with the herbs: For each cup/250 mL of olive oil, add 4 tbsp/60 mL chopped fresh rosemary, or 2 tbsp/30 mL dried herbes de Provence; add salt and pepper to taste.

Toss the vegetables separately in the olive oil mixture, just enough to coat. Place on oiled cookie sheets, spreading them out. Do not overcrowd vegetables.

Roast uncovered at 350°F/180°C for about 25 minutes. Toss and brush with a little more of the herbed oil if needed. Roast for 25 minutes longer, or until the vegetables are cooked .

Some vegetables roast more quickly than others, so check during the last 10 minutes or so and remove the cooked vegetables from the oven and set them aside in a casserole (beets usually take the longest). I usually toss all the vegetables together in the casserole once they are roasted. Serve immediately. If prepared ahead, reheat in a 350°F/180°C oven, uncovered, for about 25 minutes or until warmed.

DIANE'S SECRETS:

Herbes de Provence is a herb mixture used in many French dishes. It is an equal blend of dried oregano, thyme, marjoram and savory, and sometimes dried lavender. You can find it in specialty food shops. You can also try these vegetables with the **Quick Aioli Dip** (pg. 63).

ROASTED BEETS: I add the roasted beets to the rest of the vegetables just before serving, so they won't colour the other vegetables beet red!

FENNEL

Dried or fresh, this vegetable has a sweet licorice flavour. It's excellent with fish and chopped into soups and salads; fresh fennel stalks and their feathery leaves both are used in salads. It's also a treat to slice it thin, let it sit in ice until well chilled, then munch on it instead of celery. Try serving it with appetizers, in place of olives.

STUFFED TOMATOES À LA PROVENÇALE

Serves 6

These stuffed tomatoes go beautifully with the **Mushroom Pancake** brunch dish (pg. 142) or other egg dishes. They also go well as a side vegetable dish for poultry, meats and fish. For total comfort foods, try them with everyone's favourite, macaroni and cheese! These tomatoes are best made early on the morning of serving. Leave at room temperature: Do not refrigerate.

3	large tomatoes, cut in half widthwise	3
1 cup	soft bread crumbs	250 mL
1/4 cup	grated Parmesan cheese	60 mL
1	large clove garlic, crushed (optional)	1
1 tbsp	fresh basil, finely chopped	15 mL
	OR	
1/2 tsp	herbes de Provence	2.5 mL
	salt, pepper to taste	
3 tbsp	olive oil	45 mL

METHOD:

With your fingers, remove the excess seeds from the tomatoes, keeping the fruit intact. To prevent the tomatoes from becoming too soggy when baking, turn them upside down on paper towels for a few minutes to drain the excess juices. Pat dry.

Blend together remaining ingredients. Place tomatoes in a lightly oiled casserole; don't overcrowd. Top each tomato half with an equal portion of the bread crumbs, pressing down slightly. Sprinkle a little Parmesan cheese on top of each tomato half.

Bake at 350°F/180°C for about 25 minutes, or until the tomatoes are warm and the topping is golden.

POMMES PARISIENNE

Serves 4

These classic French-style potatoes are cooked with minimum fat and boast only 117 calories per serving. The potatoes can be partially prepared a day ahead.

4	medium potatoes, peeled and soaked in ice water	4
1 tsp	butter	5 mL
½ tsp	safflower oil	2.5 mL
3 tbsp	chopped parsley	45 mL
	salt and pepper to taste	

METHOD:

A day ahead, shape out enough potato balls with a melon cutter to allow about five per person. Keep in bowl of ice water to prevent discoloration. When all balls are made, drop them into a pot of boiling water and simmer for about 2 minutes. Drain, cool and store, covered, in the refrigerator.

TO SERVE:

Heat the butter and oil in a non-stick skillet. Add the potato balls and toss back and forth for about 5 minutes, or until they are golden all over and completely cooked. Add the chopped parsley, salt and pepper just before serving.

DIANE'S SECRETS:

Try adding a little freshly chopped dill to the potatoes.

WILLIAMS'
MEXICAN RICE

Serves 6–8

When Olympian Lynn Williams serves her famous **Cal-Mex Chicken Fiesta** entrée (pg. 184) she always includes this rice dish. It can be made a day ahead and reheated.

2 tbsp	**olive oil**	30 mL
1 cup	**chopped onions**	250 mL
2 cups	**uncooked white rice**	500 mL
2	**cloves garlic, finely chopped**	2
1 cup	**chopped red peppers,**	250 mL
	or a combination of red and yellow	
1 cup	**tomatoes, seeded,**	250 mL
	chopped	
2	**jalapeno peppers, seeded,**	2
	finely chopped	
	OR	
1/8 tsp	**dried red chili peppers**	.5 mL
2 tsp	**chili powder, or to taste**	10 mL
	salt, pepper to taste	
3 ½ cups	**boiling water**	875 mL

METHOD:

Heat the oil in a large casserole and sauté the onions until soft. Stir in the rice and garlic, cook until the rice turns transparent. Add the rest of the ingredients. Cover and cook over low heat until the rice is tender, about 25 minutes. Serve immediately, or cool, put into a casserole, refrigerate, later reheating in a 350°F/180°C oven for 25–30 minutes, or until hot.

SINGAPOREAN SPICY ASPARAGUS WITH SHIITAKE MUSHROOM SAUCE

Serves 6

This dish is a perfect accompaniment to **Pork Tenderloin Superb** (pg. 195) and **Oriental Fried Vegetable Rice** (pg. 114) or **Thai Rice** (pg. 115)

2 tbsp	vegetable or peanut oil	30 mL
4	cloves garlic, finely chopped	4
5	green onions, sliced finely on the diagonal, about 1/3 cup/80 mL	5
3-inch	piece fresh ginger, peeled, finely chopped, about 3 tbsp/45 mL	7.5-cm
3 cups	shiitake mushrooms, stemmed, sliced in half (in quarters if large)	750 mL
¼ cup	soy sauce	60 mL
¼ cup	Chinese rice wine	60 mL
¾ cup	vegetable or chicken stock	175 mL
3 tbsp	pure sesame oil	45 mL
1 tbsp	sugar	15 mL
1 tsp	red pepper oil	5 mL
	(see Oriental Noodle Salad, pg. 102)	
¼ tsp	Chinese 5-spice powder	1 mL
	pinch of red pepper flakes	
1 ½ tsp	cornstarch, blended with 1 tbsp/15 mL water	20 mL
3 lb	fresh asparagus, ends trimmed, blanched, about 4 per person	1350 g
3 tbsp	toasted sesame seeds	45 mL

METHOD:

Just before serving, in a large skillet, heat the oil, add the garlic, onions, ginger and mushrooms. Stir-fry a few minutes, then add the rest of the ingredients, except the asparagus and sesame seeds. Blend all the ingredients to thicken the sauce slightly. Set aside and keep warm while you blanch the asparagus. (You can also prepare the sauce on the morning of serving, then refrigerate.) Reheat in a skillet.

In a large sauté pan add about 1 in/2.5 cm of water and bring to a boil. Add the asparagus and simmer for about 2 minutes, or until just crunchy: don't overcook. Drain.

TO SERVE:

Put the asparagus on a large platter, pour over it the warm shiitake sauce, sprinkle the sesame seeds over all. Serve immediately.

Chinese rice wine is made from fermented rice and millet. You may use French vermouth as a substitute.

Brunch

PORTOBELLO EGGS BENNY "DOWN UNDER"

Serves 4

When I ask my family what they would like for Sunday brunch, they usually request Eggs Benny! So for New Year's Day brunch, during our holidays on the Gold Coast of Australia in 2001, I decided to try a little "down under" twist on the classic Benny. Doug and I had an eggs-with-portobello-mushroom dish at an Aussie bistro on our arrival, which gave me the idea for this Australian Benny. Rand did the grilling while I whipped up the sauce and poached the eggs, and the "family affair" brought raves from everyone. Round out the brunch with a basket of croissants, bagels, cream cheese and a platter of seasonal fruit and juices. For that special celebration, go for OJ and champagne!

4	extra thick portobello mushrooms, stems removed, brushed clean	4
16	fresh asparagus spears, ends trimmed, blanched 2 minutes or grilled	16
4	slices of tomato (1/2 in /1.25 cm thick)	4
4	large eggs, poached	4

LEMON HERB MARINADE:

	zest of 1 lemon, finely chopped	
	juice of 1 lemon	
½ tsp	Dijon mustard	2.5 mL
1	clove garlic, pressed	1
	salt and pepper to taste	
½ tsp	fresh oregano, finely chopped	2.5 mL
½ tsp	fresh thyme, finely chopped	2.5 mL
¼ cup	olive oil	60 mL

METHOD:

In a small bowl, whisk the marinade ingredients, adding the olive oil slowly. Can be made a day ahead. Refrigerate.

QUICK HOLLANDAISE SAUCE:

1 ½ cups	**mayonnaise**	375 mL
½ cup	**sour cream**	125 mL
2 tbsp	**lemon juice**	30 mL
1 tsp	**Dijon mustard**	5 mL
	salt and pepper to taste	

METHOD:

Combine ingredients. You can also make the hollandaise a day or two ahead of serving and refrigerate. On the day of serving, take it out of the refrigerator in early morning, put in a small saucepan, stir over low heat until just warmed. Do not overheat, or the sauce will separate. Set aside.

In a bowl, drizzle a little of the marinade over the portobellos to coat evenly. Set aside. Place the asparagus and tomato in a shallow dish and coat lightly with the marinade. Marinate for about 10 minutes. Set aside.

DIANE'S SECRETS:

TO GRILL: You can use an outdoor barbecue or a grill pan on top of the stove to prepare the vegetables. Just don't overcook them.

TO ROAST IN THE OVEN: Set the oven to 400°F/200°C. Place the asparagus and mushrooms on a greased cookie sheet. Roast for about 10 minutes; watch the mushrooms, as they soften quickly. Add the tomatoes for the last 5 minutes.

TO SERVE:

Grill the mushrooms, asparagus and tomatoes a few minutes. The mushrooms will take a little longer, so put them on the grill first. Set aside and keep warm while you poach the eggs.

Place one mushroom on each of four large plates. Top each with 4 spears of asparagus, a tomato slice and a poached egg. Top with a dab of the hollandaise sauce. If there is any remaining marinade, drizzle a little around the edges of the plates. Garnish with a few sprigs of oregano and thyme.

MORRIS AND KEN'S BANANA PANCAKES WITH CARAMEL-PEANUT BUTTER SAUCE

Makes about 18 (4 in / 10 cm) medium pancakes

This recipe is a collaboration of my family's "Gold Medal Pancake" recipe and Chef Lisa Rowsan's caramel-peanut butter sauce. It's dynamite!

For one of my Global "Saturday Chefs" series segments I had fun whipping up these pancakes with the genius award-winning playwright and actor Morris Panych. His partner Ken MacDonald, another genius, award-winning stage designer and artist, loves pancakes, so I'm dedicating this recipe to them both!

These are very rich and should be saved for a special brunch. Let everyone pitch in and make their own pancakes. Serve with a platter of seasonal fruit.

PANCAKE BATTER:

2 cups	flour	500 mL
1 tsp	baking soda	5 mL
	pinch of salt	
2 tbsp	white sugar	30 mL
2	large eggs, slightly beaten	2
2 cups	buttermilk	500 mL
2 tbsp	melted butter	30 mL
3–4	ripe bananas, sliced 1/4 in / .5 cm thick	3–4

METHOD:

Combine the dry ingredients in a bowl. Add the eggs, buttermilk and melted butter, stir only until the flour is barely moistened; batter will have a few lumps. Let sit for at least 30 minutes. Have ready a lightly greased hot griddle or sauté pan. For uniform pancakes, use a 1/4 cup / 60 mL measure, pour onto the skillet and place one or 2 slices of banana in the middle of each pancake. Grill until bubbles begin, about 1 minute. Flip over and grill until golden brown, about 2 minutes more. Should be golden both sides. Keep them warm in the oven while you finish the rest.

CARAMEL-PEANUT BUTTER SAUCE:

¼ cup	**butter**	60 mL
½ cup	**brown sugar**	125 mL
½ cup	**whipping cream**	125 mL
½ cup	**creamy peanut butter**	125 mL
1 tsp	**vanilla**	5 mL

METHOD:

In a small saucepan over very low heat, melt the butter. Add the brown sugar and blend well. Add the cream and vanilla, blending well. Gently whisk in the peanut butter until just smooth, stir constantly for a few minutes until the sauce is slightly thickened and creamy. Take off the heat while you prepare the pancakes. If the heat is too high, the sauce will separate.

TO SERVE:

Put 2–3 on a plate, drizzle with the warm sauce and garnish with slices of banana.

DIANE'S SECRETS:

A long, brisk walk after *this* pancake breakfast would ease the guilt of over-indulging, but it's worth it once in a while!

LINDA'S CARAMEL APPLE FRENCH TOAST

Serves 6-8

Tom and Linda Atkinson are the owners and hosts of a delightful bed and breakfast, named "Abbot On The Lake," in Kelowna, B.C. Their stately lakeshore Tudor-style home is on Okanagan Lake and their garden has won numerous awards. Tom is the talented gardener and Linda the superb cook, a dynamic team. Her breakfast table is laden with fresh berries and fruit from Okanagan orchards and flowers from their own garden. Linda's French toast is one of her signature morning treats for their pampered guests. The French bread is layered with a caramel-pecan sauce and caramelized apple slices. It's prepared the evening before, refrigerated overnight and baked just before serving, which is ideal for weekend entertaining. It's rich, so start with small servings. Enjoy it with plenty of seasonal fruit.

CARAMEL SAUCE:

1 cup	brown sugar	250 mL
½ cup	butter	125 mL
2 tbsp	light corn syrup	30 mL
1 cup	toasted pecans, chopped	250 mL

METHOD:

Place the brown sugar, butter and corn syrup together into a Teflon-coated pan and cook over medium heat until thickened, stirring constantly for 3–4 minutes. Pour into a greased 9 × 11 in / 22.5 × 27.5 mL glass dish and spread evenly over the bottom. Sprinkle the pecans over the caramel sauce.

FRENCH TOAST:

12	slices French bread,	12
	(about 1/2-in / 1.25-cm slices)	
8	large apples, peeled, thinly sliced	8
2 tsp	cinnamon	10 mL
2 tbsp	brown sugar	30 mL
6	eggs	6
1 ½ cups	milk	375 mL
2 tsp	cinnamon	10 mL
1 tsp	nutmeg	5 mL
	pure maple syrup	
	French vanilla yogurt	

METHOD:

Place 6 slices of the French bread evenly over the pecans. In a fry pan, sauté the thinly sliced apples until slightly softened, adding cinnamon and brown sugar. Place the apple slices evenly over the bread.

Beat the eggs and milk together. Pour half of the egg mixture over the apples. Now place another layer of French bread (6 slices) over the apples. Pour remaining egg mixture over the bread slices. Cover with plastic wrap and refrigerate overnight.

Just before serving, sprinkle with the remaining cinnamon and nutmeg and bake uncovered for about 40 minutes at 325°F/160°C, or until the French toast is firm. Slice into 6–8 pieces and serve each piece upside down.

Serve with pure maple syrup, warmed, and French vanilla yogurt.

GIANT DUTCH BABY
PANCAKE

Serves 4–6, depending on the appetites!
The classic Dutch Baby Pancake recipe calls for a considerable amount of butter and cream. This version uses butter only sparingly, substitutes skim milk and is only 300 calories per serving. If you want to make it richer you can use ⅓ cup/80 mL butter and whole milk. Use one large or two smaller skillets, shallow and ovenproof.

¼ cup	butter, melted	60 mL
6	eggs	6
1 ½ cups	skim milk	375 mL
1 tsp	vanilla	5 mL
1 ½ cups	flour	375 mL

METHOD:

Heat the oven to 425°F/220°C. Pour the butter into a large pan or smaller pans and place them in the oven. In a food processor or blender, whip the eggs together for a few minutes, then add the milk and vanilla, then the flour, a little at a time, blending continuously until the mixture is smooth. Don't overbeat. Pour the batter into the pans and bake on bottom rack for 10–15 minutes; add warmed applesauce spread in an even layer, and continue cooking for 10 minutes or until puffy and golden brown. Or leave plain and pass the applesauce separately.

The pancake will collapse a little as soon as you bring it out of the oven, so serve it immediately, cut into wedges with a little sprinkle of nutmeg, cinnamon and icing sugar. Let your guests add pure maple syrup and a dollop of French vanilla yogurt; serve with a platter of seasonal fruit. For a change, make the pancake with thin slices of bananas layered on the batter before baking. It's also delicious with fresh strawberries.

DUTCH BABY APPLESAUCE:			METHOD:
4 cups	green apples, thinly sliced	1 L	Mix all together in a large saucepan and cook
1 tbsp	apple juice	15 mL	gently until apples are soft. Set aside. Serve
1 tbsp	brown sugar	15 mL	separately or spread on pancake during baking.
¼ tsp	cinnamon	1 mL	Can be made a day ahead, refrigerated and
⅛ tsp	nutmeg	.5 mL	reheated just before using.

DIANE'S SECRETS:

Make the pancake batter an hour or two before baking, which results in a lighter pancake.

MUSHROOM PANCAKE

Serves 4

This pancake is similar to the Dutch Baby Pancake, but uses mushrooms instead of fruit; I like to use a combination of portobello, shiitake, oyster, button or cremini. The pancake is baked in the oven just before serving and I like to accompany it with the tart Green Onion Sauce, European back bacon and **Stuffed Tomatoes à la Provençale** (pg. 128). After a brisk Sunday walk, run or cycle or just after catching up on all the week's papers, this menu hits the spot!

MUSHROOM MIXTURE:

4 tbsp	butter	60 mL
5 cups	button or assorted mushrooms, sliced	1.25 L
½ cup	shallots, chopped	125 mL
	salt and pepper to taste	

METHOD:

Just before serving, in a skillet melt 2 tbsp/30 mL butter. Add the mushrooms and shallots and sauté for a few minutes, until softened. Add salt and pepper to taste. Set aside.

BATTER:

4	large eggs	4
1 ¼ cups	milk	310 mL
¾ cup	flour + pinch salt	175 mL
½ cup	Parmesan cheese	125 mL

In a medium-size bowl of an electric mixer, beat the eggs and milk. Gradually add the flour and a pinch of salt. Blend until smooth. Refrigerate for at least 30 minutes before baking.

GREEN ONION SAUCE:

⅓ cup	plain yogurt	80 mL
½ cup	sour cream	125 mL
2 tbsp	green onions or chives, finely chopped	30 mL
1 ½ tbsp	grainy Dijon mustard	20 mL
1 ½ tbsp	olive oil	20 mL
	salt and pepper to taste	

In a bowl, combine all the ingredients and blend well. Can be made a day ahead, and can be served at room temperature or slightly warmed.

Just before serving, set the oven at 400°F/200°C. Spoon the remaining 2 tbsp/30 mL butter in a 10-in/25-cm ovenproof skillet and put into the oven until melted. Remove hot pan from the oven and add the mushrooms and shallots mixture. Pour the egg batter evenly over the top of the mushrooms. Sprinkle the Parmesan cheese over all. Bake on the bottom rack for 25–30 minutes or until puffy and golden. Serve with Green Onion Sauce.

FRITTATA PRIMAVERA

Serves 6

This hearty frittata is great for weekend brunches. It has a soufflé texture with the addition of bread cubes and lots of cheese. It takes a little time to prepare the vegetables, but is worth the effort.

VEGETABLE MIXTURE:

3 tbsp	**olive oil**	45 mL
½ cup	**red onions, finely chopped**	125 mL
3	**cloves garlic, finely chopped**	3
	medium zucchini, chopped into small cubes (about 2 1/2 cups / 625 mL)	
1 cup	**fresh mushrooms, coarsely chopped**	250 mL
1	**each small red and yellow peppers, seeded and finely chopped**	1
	pinch of red pepper flakes	

METHOD:

In a large fry pan, combine the first seven ingredients, sauté for a few minutes. Drain well. Set aside.

DIANE'S SECRETS:

This frittata can be made a day or two ahead, leaving out the tomato-cheese topping, and kept in the refrigerator. For a larger crowd, double the recipe and fill two springform pans. Bring frittata to room temperature, cover well with tinfoil and reheat in 350°F/180°C oven for about 30 minutes, or until heated through. This dish does not freeze well: best served fresh!

EGG MIXTURE:

6	**large eggs, slightly beaten**	6
¼ cup	**milk**	60 mL
	salt and pepper to taste	
2 cups	**day-old French bread,**	500 mL
	cut into small cubes	
8 oz	**cream cheese, cut into**	200 mL
	small cubes	
2 cups	**grated Swiss cheese**	500 mL
	(Gruyère or Emmenthal)	
3 tbsp	**Parmesan cheese**	45 mL

TOPPING:

5–6	**Roma tomatoes, sliced thinly**	5–6
3 tbsp	**Parmesan cheese**	45 mL

METHOD:

In a large bowl, combine the eggs, milk, salt, pepper, bread cubes and cheeses except for the Parmesan. Stir in the vegetable mixture and blend well. Pour into a greased 10-inch/25-cm springform pan. Pat down mixture to make an even layer. Wrap the outside of the pan with foil to prevent leaks. Sprinkle top with 3 tbsp/45 mL Parmesan cheese.

Put on a cookie sheet and bake at 350°F/180°C oven for 40–45 minutes, or until golden and firm in the middle.

Just before serving, take from oven and cover top with the sliced Roma tomatoes; sprinkle Parmesan cheese over the tomatoes. Return to the oven for 5 minutes.

EGGS SANTA FE

Serves 8

This is another weekend brunch dish Doug and I enjoyed at a quaint Santa Fe restaurant many years ago. The owner of the restaurant shared his secret ingredients with me and it's a change from the usual Eggs Ranchero. Pick up the condiments from a Mexican deli and you're ahead of the game!

10	eggs	10
1 pt	creamy cottage cheese	475 mL
½ cup	flour, (blended with	125 mL
	1 tsp/5 mL baking powder,	
	1/2 tsp/2.5 mL salt)	
¼ cup	melted butter	60 mL
1 lb	cheddar,	450 g
	Monterey Jack or Swiss cheese	
	(or a combination of any 2)	
8 oz	canned chopped	100 g
	green chilies, drained,	
	OR	
4	jalapeno peppers, seeded,	4
	finely chopped	
	dash Tabasco	
	pepper to taste	

CONDIMENTS:

guacamole or sliced ripe avocados

salsa

sour cream

chopped green onions

tortilla chips or warmed flour tortillas

METHOD:

In a bowl, whisk the eggs and cottage cheese to blend well. Slowly whisk in the rest of the ingredients. Pour into a greased 9 × 13-in /22.5 × 32.5-cm casserole and bake in a 350°F/180°C oven for 35–45 minutes, or until firm and golden.

TO SERVE:

Spoon some of the eggs onto the serving plates, let your guests help themselves to the condiments.

DIANE'S SECRETS:

Try adding a cup of chopped shrimp, chicken or ham to the basic egg dish.

THE MAJESTIC SOUFFLÉ

Soufflés are back! Restaurants all over North America are again featuring them on their menus, from a first course to a dramatic grande finale. They appear to be temperamental and a lot of fuss to make, but they are really not that difficult. Soufflés are a perfect choice for a luncheon or weekend brunch when entertaining. I love to serve them as a first course before a special dinner party.

Here are some tips for successful soufflés. Once you perfect making them, they will become one of your own signature dishes!

- ～ Have the egg whites at room temperature.

- ～ Use a very clean metal or glass mixing bowl (metal is the best). Make sure there are no specks of oil of any kind on the surface. Avoid plastic bowls — they attract grease.

- ～ Beat the whites slowly at first, creating lots of bubbles.

- ～ Use a good strong electric beater or a balloon-type wire whisk.

- ～ Once the egg whites start to hold their peaks and are smooth and creamy you are ready to fold in the rest of the ingredients. The whites should be stiff but still moist. Do not overbeat.

- ～ The soufflé dish should be well greased and dusted with bread crumbs or grated Parmesan cheese (or sugar for a dessert soufflé). The coating allows the mixture to cling to the dish and rise high. After coating the dish, chill it in the refrigerator: A cold dish will help the soufflé rise evenly.

~ Prepare the base sauce and have ready at room temperature before you beat the whites. You can make the sauce a day ahead and refrigerate. Bring to room temperature. Then fold the whites gently into the sauce mixture, adding a little at a time. Pour into the cold soufflé dish and pop into the oven.

~ Don't open the oven door to check on the soufflé's progress, or it will fall. When cooked, the soufflé should be golden and firm to the touch.

~ A good soufflé is worth waiting for. Make sure the guests are ready to eat as soon as you bring the soufflé to the table.

~ Preheat the oven to 400°F/200°C, then reduce to 375°F/190°C just before you put in the soufflé.

~ Just before popping the soufflés into the oven, run your finger around the rim of the dish to help the soufflés rise.

~ Soufflés can be made completely and kept in the fridge for up to 2 hours before baking. Cook for 5 minutes longer if you do this.

~ Twice-baked cheese soufflés are the latest favourites with many chefs. Bake the soufflés a day ahead. Cool and refrigerate; they will fall slightly. To serve, bring the soufflés to room temperature. Preheat the oven to 400°F/200°C. Turn the soufflés into individual shallow ovenproof ramekin dishes. Pour a little whipping cream over the top of each, sprinkle some Parmesan cheese on top and bake for 10–15 minutes, or until golden. Serve immediately.

~ The best method is still to bake them just before serving, but if preparation time is a factor the twice-baked soufflés would be fine.

CHÈVRE SOUFFLÉ

Serves 8 as first course

These soufflés are divine! I fill the centres of each with additional crumbled goat cheese, which makes them very creamy. They are teasing starters for that special dinner party!

SAUCE:

¼ cup	butter	60 mL
¼ cup	flour	60 mL
1 cup	hot milk	250 mL
3 oz	chèvre, crumbled	75 g
2	cloves garlic, pressed	2
1 tsp	olive oil	5 mL
	salt and pepper to taste	
1 tbsp	green onions or chives, finely chopped	15 mL
½ tsp	fresh thyme, finely chopped	125 mL
3	egg yolks, slightly beaten	3

METHOD:

In a saucepan, melt the butter over medium heat. Add the flour, cook, whisking constantly for 1–2 minutes. Gradually whisk in the hot milk. Bring to a simmer and cook until the sauce begins to thicken and is smooth, about 3 minutes. Remove from heat and stir in two-thirds of the chèvre, blending well. In a small bowl, mash together the garlic and oil. Add to the sauce, with salt and pepper to taste. Cover with plastic wrap and set aside to cool. Can be made a day or two ahead of serving and refrigerated.

Just before baking the soufflés, gently rewarm the sauce. Fold in the onions, thyme and egg yolks. Cool. Set aside while you prepare the ramekins.

RAMEKINS:			METHOD:
	butter		Just before baking, butter 8 (4-oz/100-g) ramekins
8 tsp	**grated Parmesan cheese**	40 g	and coat each with 1 tsp/5 mL Parmesan cheese. Set aside.

SOUFFLÉS:			METHOD:
3	**egg whites**	3	Up to 2 hours before baking, in a large bowl beat
8 tsp	**Parmesan cheese**	40 g	the egg whites until stiff but not dry. Fold one-quarter of the egg whites into the chèvre mixture, then fold into the remaining egg whites.

Fill the prepared ramekins with half the soufflé mixture. Divide the remaining one-third of the chèvre evenly among the ramekins and cover with the rest of the mixture. Run your finger around the rims and sprinkle tops with 1 tsp/5 mL Parmesan cheese each.

Can be refrigerated for up to 2 hours. A half hour before baking, set the oven to 400°F/200°C.

DIANE'S SECRETS:

I like to make the soufflé batter up to 2 hours before baking and refrigerate it until ready to pop into the oven. It works beautifully.

If you would like a sweeter garlic flavour, rub a little oil on the 2 cloves of garlic, wrap in tinfoil, roast in the oven for about 30 minutes, or until soft. Mash with the 1 tsp/5 mL of oil and fold into the soufflé mixture.

TO SERVE:

Put the ramekins in a large pan. Pour in 1–2 in/2.5–5 cm of hot water. Turn the oven down to 375°F/190°C. Bake until the soufflés are puffed and golden brown, 25–30 minutes. Serve immediately.

FRESH CRAB SOUFFLÉ

Serves 4

Elegant and airy, this soufflé adds a sophisticated note to brunch or a light dinner. Equally delectable with fresh shrimp!

CHEESE SAUCE:

¼ cup	butter	60 mL
¼ cup	flour	60 mL
1 cup	warm milk	250 mL
3 tbsp	green onions or chives, finely chopped	45 mL
	salt and pepper to taste	
¼ tsp	Dijon mustard	60 mL
½ cup	grated Gruyère or Emmenthal cheese	125 mL
4	egg yolks, slightly beaten	4
1 cup	fresh crabmeat, picked over for shell, or 1 cup / 250mL cooked shrimp, chopped	250 mL

METHOD:

In a small saucepan, melt the butter, add flour, whisk for a few minutes, then remove from heat and gradually whisk in the warm milk. Return to low heat and continue to stir until the mixture is thickened and smooth.

Add the onions, salt and pepper to taste, mustard and cheese and stir until cheese is melted. This sauce can be made a day ahead, cooled and refrigerated.

Just before baking, gently rewarm the sauce and fold in the egg yolks. Set aside to cool. Fold in the crabmeat or shrimp.

SOUFFLÉ:

5	**egg whites**	5
3 tbsp	**grated Parmesan cheese**	45 mL

SOUFFLÉ DISH:

Just before baking, prepare a 1 ½-qt / 1 ½-L dish by buttering and coating with grated Parmesan cheese, then chilling. Or you can prepare 8 (½-cup / 250 mL) ramekins if you would like individual soufflés as a starter course.

Preheat the oven to 400°F / 200°C.

METHOD:

Up to 2 hours before baking, beat the egg whites until stiff, but not dry, and fold a little at a time into the crab mixture. Pour into the soufflé dish or ramekins. Sprinkle top with Parmesan cheese. Put the soufflé dish or ramekins into a larger pan, pour in 1–2 in / 2.5–5 cm of hot water. Turn oven down to 375°F / 190°C and bake the soufflé for 35–40 minutes or until firm and golden. The individual soufflés may take less time. Serve immediately.

BREAK AN EGG!

Everyone can make scrambled eggs, but an omelette is something else! It's a challenge, an intriguing creation. And it must be done well.

DIANE'S SECRETS TO A GOOD OMELETTE:

- ~ The pan is important. A good Teflon pan works well, preferably about 10 in/25 cm in diameter, though you could use two 6-in/15-cm pans. Heat to just the right temperature: if a small lump of cold butter placed into the pan sizzles briskly without browning, then the pan is ready.

- ~ Do not beat the eggs for too long. In fact, don't use an egg beater at all: it takes all the life out of the eggs, leaving them thin and tough when cooked. Thirty seconds with a good strong fork is ample beating for 6 eggs.

- ~ Do not add pepper to the eggs before cooking. Pepper will discolour and toughen the eggs.

- ~ One tbsp of butter in the pan is enough for a 3–6-egg omelette. Let the butter come to a froth, wait until the bubbles burst, then pour in the eggs.

- ~ Stir for just a second with the flat of a fork. Let the omelette cook; lift the eggs here and there to let the liquid run underneath. If you are folding the omelette, bring the left half to the centre while the centre is still soft, but make the third fold as you slide it out onto the serving plate.

- ~ For a basic omelette for two people you will need 6 eggs, 2 tbsp/30 mL water, pepper, salt and 2 tbsp/30 mL butter.

SPANISH OMELETTE

Some of the best omelettes Doug and I have eaten were in Spain, and the Tortilla De Patatas is perfection! Each restaurant offers its own version of this classic dish and it is served at all hours of the day. We had our first Spanish omelette at 11:30 p.m., not a.m.!

2	medium potatoes, cut in half lengthwise (or 5 small)	2
1 tbsp	olive oil	15 mL
½ cup	onions, chopped	125 mL
	salt to taste	
6	extra-large eggs	
1 tbsp	cold water	15 mL
	pepper to taste	
¼ cup	Manchego or Parmesan cheese, grated	60 mL
2	cloves garlic, pressed (optional)	2

METHOD:

Peel and slice the potatoes as thinly as possible; a mandolin is great for this. Heat the oil in a non-stick, 10-in/25-cm pan (or use two 6-in/15-cm pans). Add the potatoes, onions and garlic; sauté over medium heat until golden. Cover, reduce heat to low and cook until tender, about 10 minutes, stirring frequently to prevent sticking. Make sure the potatoes are cooked before adding the eggs. Add salt to taste. Beat eggs lightly with the flat side of a fork, add the cold water and pour into the potato-onion mixture. Stir for just a second with the flat side of a fork. Cook the omelette, lifting the eggs to let the liquid run underneath. Continue to cook until the eggs are set. Sprinkle with pepper and the cheese.

DIANE'S SECRETS:

Manchego is one of Spain's best-known cheeses. It is made from sheep's milk and may be available from specialty cheese shops. Parmesan cheese may be substituted.

Cover the pan with a large plate and hold in place with one hand. Quickly turn the pan upside down so the omelette falls onto the plate. Slide the omelette back into the pan or pans. Cook for a few minutes more to lightly brown the bottom. Slide onto serving plates. Serve with **Tomato Salsa** (pg. 154).

TOMATO RELISH
FOR TORTILLA DE PATATAS

Makes about 1 cup/250 mL

			METHOD:
¾ cup	**fresh tomatoes, chopped**	175 mL	
¼ cup	**shallots or purple**	60 mL	
	onions, finely chopped		
½ cup	**white baby corn or**	125 mL	
	yellow (canned)		
1	**clove garlic, pressed**	1	
1	**small jalapeno pepper, seeded**	1	
	and finely chopped		
	pinch each of salt and pepper		
	pinch of sugar		
1 tsp	**white wine or sherry vinegar**	5 mL	
1 tsp	**water**	5 mL	

METHOD:

Blend all ingredients together well. Can be made a day ahead and refrigerated. Serve at room temperature, or slightly warmed.

BASQUE
OMELETTE

Serves 4–6

This is another version of the Spanish Omelette and its tasty ham-and-vegetable filling can be made well ahead of time. Make a plain omelette in the usual way, using 6 eggs (pg. 152). Spread the sauce in the middle, fold in half and turn out onto a hot serving platter.

2 tbsp	olive oil	30 mL
1	small onion, white or purple, chopped	1
1	red pepper, finely chopped	1
1	clove garlic, pressed	1
1	ham slice (1/4 in / .5 cm) thick, cut into long strips)	1
2	fresh tomatoes, seeded, diced	2
1 tbsp	each of fresh basil and thyme, chopped	15 mL

METHOD:

Heat the oil in a fry pan and add the onion, pepper and garlic. Stir over high heat for about 2 minutes, until softened. Add the ham, sauté for about 3 minutes. Add the tomatoes, simmer on low for about 10 minutes or until the sauce is thick. Add the fresh herbs, salt and pepper to taste.

OTHER OMELETTE SUGGESTIONS:

To the basic 6-egg omelette, add sautéed mushrooms, regular or wild, grated Asiago or Monterey Jack cheese. Add smoked salmon and chopped chives or green onions, top with a little sour cream or chèvre. For Mexican style, add seeded, chopped jalapeno peppers, sliced avocado, grated Monterey Jack cheese, topped with sour cream and Mexican salsa.

--- T H Y M E ---

Usually combined with marjoram for flavouring soups and vinaigrettes and is one of the plants used in herbes de Provence. Thyme is one herb that is acceptable when dried.

Main Courses

Seafood

PRINCELY PRAWNS

Serves 6

I am often asked when giving cooking classes, "What is a prawn, and what is a shrimp?" The two words are used interchangeably. Some chefs say the difference is their size: that small and medium shrimp are sold simply as "shrimp," while large, extra-large and jumbo shrimp are called "prawns." You say shrimp, I say prawns — whatever you prefer to call this delectable shellfish, they are "princely"!

What more could you ask for on a balmy summer evening than a "prawn feed" with lots of salad. **Salade St.-Tropez** (pg. 84) or **Tropical Salad** (pg. 93) would complement the shrimp. Add some baguettes and a choice of wine or beer and let the party begin.

This simple quick method of preparing prawns comes from Liz and Jack Bryan, original publishers of my Chef on the Run cookbook series. The garlic-wine sauce in which the prawns cook is really more than adequate as a dipping sauce for them, but it's fun to have a selection of dips such as **Quick Lemon Dill Mayonnaise** (pg. 63), **Creole Tartar Sauce** (pg. 64) and **Soy-Honey Dipping Sauce** (pg. 66). Allow about ½–¾ lb / 225–340 g of prawns per person. About half the weight is lost in the shell.

3 ¾–4 lb	**medium-size whole raw prawns**	1.7–1.8 kg
½ cup	**butter**	125 mL
3	**cloves garlic, pressed**	3
	pinch of salt and pepper	
½ cup	**dry white wine**	125 mL

METHOD:

The prawns must be cooked at the very last minute, but this is not a problem as they take mere minutes. Heat the butter in a large skillet. Add the garlic, salt and pepper, then add the prawns and stir over medium heat for about one minute. Add the wine, mix well. Don't overcook, or the prawns will be mushy. The whole procedure should take only 3–4 minutes. Stir once during the cooking. Serve the garlic-wine cooking liquid for dipping.

These prawns can be served with heads on or off, but they must be cooked and served in their shells for best flavour.

SHRIMP ISTANBUL

Serves 6

This dish has to be one of the all-time classics of the Chef on the Run series. It appeared in the first book, *Chef on the Run*, and it's still a family tradition to serve Shrimp Istanbul for a birthday or special celebration dinner. Quick to make and usually served with rice, it's a perfect addition to any buffet or as a main entrée on its own.

4 tbsp	**butter**	60 mL
1 ½ cups	**mushrooms, sliced**	375 mL
1	**medium white onion, finely chopped**	1
1 lb	**fresh cooked baby shrimp**	450 g
	(hand-peeled are best)	
¼ cup	**medium dry sherry**	60 mL
2 tbsp	**tomato paste**	30 mL
1 ½ cups	**light cream**	375 mL
4 tbsp	**cornstarch**	60 mL
½ cup	**half-and-half**	125 mL
½ cup	**sour cream**	125 mL

METHOD:

In a medium skillet, sauté the onions and mushrooms in butter until slightly tender, about 3 minutes. Remove from pan and set aside. Add the shrimp to the same pan and sauté for about 2 minutes. Add the sherry. Blend the tomato paste with the light cream, then add to the shrimp, blending well. Add the cooked onions and mushrooms and simmer slowly for about 5 minutes. Blend together the cornstarch and the half-and-half, add to the shrimp mixture and stir gently, simmering, until the mixture is thickened. Fold in the sour cream and turn into a 1 ½-qt / 1 ½-L casserole. Refrigerate for up to 24 hours.

DIANE'S SECRETS:

Shrimp Istanbul freezes well. Remove from the freezer the night before serving and thaw in the refrigerator. Sometimes freezing thins the sauce. If this happens, just add 1 tbsp / 15 mL of cornstarch blended with a little half-and-half. The sauce should be just thin enough to pour.

TO SERVE:

Bake, covered, in a 350°F / 180°C oven for 40–45 minutes or until hot. Remove cover for the final 15 minutes, stir until smooth. Serve over rice.

GARY'S BBQ SALMON FILLET WITH SUN-DRIED TOMATO MARINADE

Serves 6–8

Gary Winkelman is in charge of the salmon barbecue at the post-Harry Jerome Classic track meet party hosted by Ken Elmer and Jan Neufeld in their heritage home in New Westminster. Gary's secret is his marinade of red onions, garlic and sun-dried tomatoes. The salmon melts in your mouth, it's so moist! The athletes from all over the world who compete in our Harry Jerome Classic line up for a taste of Gary's salmon and it quickly disappears: his record is 75 salmon for the volunteers at the post-meet party. The only complaint he receives is that they want more!

Here is Gary's winning recipe, served with basmati rice or oven-roasted potatoes, and seasonal vegetables from his garden. His wife Pavlina and most athletes love garlic, so Gary adds lots of it to his marinade!

1	**salmon fillet, skin on, (about 2 lbs / 900 g)**
1	**large lemon**

GARNISH:

cilantro, parsley, or chopped fresh herbs

METHOD:

Lay out one or two layers of tinfoil on a chopping board. Fold the edges up to make a bed for the salmon. Oil the tinfoil slightly, then place the salmon skin side down on the tinfoil. Squeeze the juice of the whole lemon evenly over the entire salmon, then cover with the marinade. You can do this a few hours ahead of time and refrigerate.

Portobello Eggs Benny "Down Under" > pg. 134

Frittata Primavera > pg. 143

Papillote of Seafood with Tomatoes and Zucchini   > pg. 166

David's Chicken and Artichokes in Phyllo Paper > pg. 182

Mexican Torta (Chilaquiles)   > *pg. 186*

Lamb Shank with Orzo   > *pg. 190*

Berries in Champagne Jelly   > pg. 227

SUN-DRIED TOMATO MARINADE:

¼	**medium red onion, finely chopped**	¼
6–8	**cloves garlic, finely chopped**	6–8
1 cup	**sun-dried tomatoes in oil, finely chopped**	250 mL
	salt and pepper to taste	
2–3 tbsp	**fresh herbs (such as basil, oregano, thyme), finely chopped**	30–45 mL
¼ cup	**olive oil**	60 mL

METHOD:

In a bowl, whisk the ingredients to blend well. Set aside.

TO SERVE:

Preheat the barbecue to a medium setting. When ready, turn the heat down on the side of the barbecue on which the thin tail rests. It will take 10–14 minutes to cook the salmon and do not overcook: salmon should be just opaque. Check doneness by cutting a thin wedge down the centreline at the thick end, with a fork. Once cooked, turn the heat off immediately and transfer the salmon to a heated platter. The salmon meat will separate easily from the foil and the skin. Simply fold the tinfoil and discard. No more scraping the barbecue grill! Garnish with cilantro, parsley or fresh herbs.

GARY'S TIPS FOR THE PERFECT BBQ SALMON:

Once you know how long your particular brand of barbecue takes to cook a salmon, you can have the lid closed until it's done. This keeps the salmon extra moist.

GRILLED SALMON
AND ONIONS

Serves 8

A filleted whole salmon is marinated with just a teaser of Oriental flavourings, which the onions also pick up as they grill to a crispy brown. Serve with **Hot Potato Salad** (pg. 96) or **Oriental Fried Vegetable Rice** (pg. 114).

1	salmon fillet, skin on	1
	(about 2 lb/900 g)	
4	large purple onions, peeled,	4
	sliced into thirds	
	Lemon wedges, cilantro, parsley	
	or dill (for garnish)	

MARINADE FOR SALMON AND ONIONS:

½ cup	soy sauce	125 mL
½ cup	dry sherry or	125 mL
	sherry vinegar	
¼ cup	rice wine vinegar	60 mL
2 tbsp	sesame oil	30 mL
⅔ cup	green onions or shallots,	160 mL
	chopped	
2	cloves garlic, finely chopped	2

METHOD:

Blend marinade ingredients. Can be made a day or two ahead and refrigerated. Take out a few hours before preparing the salmon.

Two to three hours before serving, lay the salmon fillet in a large shallow casserole, skin side down. Pour over it enough of the marinade to cover before refrigerating, leaving some for the onions. Place the sliced onions in a casserole, pour over some of the marinade to cover. Leave at room temperature. Turn the salmon and onions once or twice to make sure they are well marinated. Reserve any of the remaining marinade for basting.

Oil the barbecue grill well and place over high heat (either gas or hot coals). Lay the salmon and onions on the grill and cook for 4–5 minutes on each side, basting well. The salmon should become just opaque and the onions a dark crispy golden colour.

TO SERVE:

Put the salmon and onions on a platter. Decorate with lemon wedges, sprigs of cilantro, parsley or fresh dill. Serve hot or cold.

MARCELLE'S **RED SNAPPER** WITH **SWEET PEPPERS**

Serves 6–8

Our friends Marcelle and Don McLean's red snapper entrée is a quick-to-make dinner when you are on the run. It can be prepared ahead of time and needs only last-minute steaming. The addition of chili powder, cumin and garlic powder gives this dish a good kick! Serve with **Pommes Parisienne** (pg. 129) or rice.

2 lb	**red snapper fillet**	900 g

SPICE BLEND:

2 tsp	**sweet Spanish or Hungarian paprika**	10 mL
½ tsp	**each of chili powder, cumin and garlic powder, or to taste**	2.5 mL
¼ tsp	**black pepper**	1 mL
2 tbsp	**vegetable oil**	30 mL

VEGETABLES:

5	**cloves garlic, peeled, sliced in half**	5
2	**red peppers, sliced into strips**	2
1	**yellow pepper, sliced into strips**	1
½ cup	**chopped parsley**	125 mL
¼ cup	**water**	60 mL

METHOD:

Blend the spices and pepper together, add the oil and whisk well. Roll the snapper fillets in the spice mixture and place in a non-stick pan. Roll the pepper strips in the remaining spice mixture and arrange over the snapper, sprinkle the parsley on top. Add the garlic cloves and water. Refrigerate until ready to serve.

TO SERVE:

Simmer, covered, until the liquid has evaporated and the snapper is opaque. Don't overcook.

CUMIN

Cumin is a member of the parsley family, with a slightly bitter taste. Only the seeds, which resemble those of caraway in both looks and flavour, are used in cooking. It is a basic spice for curries and Middle Eastern cuisine.

HALIBUT MANGO TANGO WITH GRILLED VEGETABLES

Serves 6

The delicate taste of freshly caught halibut is accented by a tangy mango-lime sauce. The fish is first steeped in a Japanese marinade, which is also used for the grilled vegetables. Serve with **Thai Rice with Coconut Milk** (pg. 115).

6	**6-oz/150-g pieces of halibut, boned and skinned, or sea bass**	6

MARINADE:

6 tbsp	**sake or sherry**	90 mL
6 tbsp	**soy sauce**	90 mL
3 tbsp	**pure sesame oil**	45 mL

METHOD:

Mix all ingredients and divide into two portions, one for the halibut, the other for the grilled vegetables. Marinate the halibut for 2–3 hours, turning once in a while. Have the barbecue coals as hot as possible, oil the grill well and grill the fish, allowing about 5 minutes for each ½ in /1.25 cm of thickness, measured at the thickest part. Take care not to overcook: the fish should be ready when it is no longer translucent. About 4–5 minutes per side should be enough. Serve with Mango-Lime Sauce.

GRILLED VEGETABLES:

3	**baby Japanese eggplants, split in half**	3
1	**each red and yellow peppers, cored and halved**	1
24	**snow peas (allow 4 per person)**	24
6	**large fresh shiitake or regular mushrooms, stemmed**	6

METHOD:

Blanch the snow peas in boiling water for about 30 seconds, pat dry. Marinate all the vegetables in the reserved marinade for about 30 minutes. Wrap the snow peas in heavy tinfoil, keep warm on the grill. Grill the eggplants, red peppers and shiitake mushrooms for a few minutes on each side until tender, brushing frequently with marinade. The vegetables can be cooked at the same time as the fish, if there is room on the grill. The blackened skin of the peppers can be peeled off and the peppers cut into strips for serving.

MANGO-LIME SAUCE:

2–3 **peeled and sliced ripe mangoes,** 2–3
(about 2 cups/500 mL)

OR

14 oz	**can sliced mangoes**	350 g
1 tbsp	**fresh ginger, finely chopped**	15 mL
½ cup	**chicken stock**	125 mL
2 tbsp	**lime juice**	30 mL
	zest and juice of 1 lime	
2 tbsp	**fresh orange juice**	30 mL
2 tbsp	**chopped fresh basil**	30 mL

METHOD:

Combine all the sauce ingredients in a food processor. Can be made a day ahead and refrigerated.

TO SERVE:

Heat just before serving, thinning out with more stock if the mixture is too thick. Add more basil to taste. Put a little of the sauce on a plate and top with the grilled halibut. Serve with the grilled vegetables and Thai rice.

JUST THE FACTS — WHAT SOY SAUCE DO I USE?

There are so many types of soy sauce, it can get rather confusing. Shoyu and tamari are both dark Japanese soy sauces, with a very intense flavour. Mushroom soy sauce has a distinct mushroom taste and is wonderful for stir-frying mushrooms, or to enhance a pasta with mushrooms. A little goes a long way! Kejap manis is a sweet soy sauce, used in most Indonesian cooking such as satays. When a recipe calls for a light soy sauce, that doesn't mean it is has less salt, but that it is lighter in colour. Look for a soy that distinctly states "less salt" on its label if that's what you're looking for. Yeo's and Kikkomon soy sauces work well.

PAPILLOTE OF SEAFOOD
WITH TOMATOES AND ZUCCHINI

Serves 6

The seafood in this recipe can be varied according to availability. Cooking parchment, available from kitchen boutiques, can be substituted for the aluminum foil and actually is more traditional. Be careful not to overcook the fish. Serve with steamed new baby potatoes fresh from the garden to soak up the tasty seafood juices. If time is short, replace the tomato coulis below with a good tomato sauce from your deli. This dish boasts only 76 calories per serving.

TOMATO COULIS:

4	large tomatoes, peeled, seeded and chopped (1 1/2 –2 cups / 374–500 mL)	
2	cloves garlic, finely chopped	
1/4 cup	dry white wine	60 mL
2 tbsp	basil, finely chopped	30 mL
2 tbsp	oregano, finely chopped	30 mL
	salt and pepper to taste	

METHOD:

4 In a sauté pan, combine the coulis ingredients. Simmer for 10—15 minutes, or until thickened. Can be made a day or two ahead and refrigerated.

SEAFOOD AND VEGETABLES:

18	mussels or clams, cleaned, or combination of both
5	3-in/7.5-cm pieces of red snapper or halibut, skinned
6	3-in/7.5-cm pieces of salmon, skinned
15	prawns, cleaned, unpeeled
16	mushrooms, sliced
1	zucchini, cut in half, thinly sliced into 24 strips
1	small purple or white onion, thinly sliced
1	lemon, sliced thinly and halved
6	fresh sprigs of tarragon, basil, thyme or oregano
	salt and pepper to taste

METHOD:

A few hours ahead of baking, fold into halves 6 pieces of cooking parchment or heavy aluminum foil, each about 16 × 24 in/40 × 60 cm. Cut each into a heart shape (each heart should have a fold down the middle). Open the hearts and brush with a little vegetable oil. Place 3 tbsp of the tomato coulis in the centre of each heart. Place the fish on top of the coulis and cover with 4 strips of zucchini. Arrange the rest of the ingredients around the fish. Place fresh herb sprig in the centre and sprinkle with salt and pepper to taste. Fold the halves of the hearts together and seal the open edges by rolling them into a double fold.

Place on a baking sheet and bake at 450°F/230°F for about 15 minuters, or until the mussels or clams open. Check one package after 12 minutes. Place each papillote in a large soup or pasta bowl, slit open down the centre and spread open.

Throw away any of the mussels or clams that don't open.

PACIFIC NORTHWEST
SALMON TORTE

Serves 4 as main course, 6 as appetizer

It's a winner! From *Chef on the Run*, this quick salmon torte recipe comes from Thelma and Lee Wright, two former Olympic competitors. Whip it up for lunch or dinner, or in small wedges for an appetizer course. For a main course add a green salad. I like to use smoked salmon or leftover baked or grilled salmon, but in a pinch canned salmon is fine.

CRUST:

1 cup	whole wheat flour	250 mL
⅔ cup	grated cheddar cheese	160 mL
¼ cup	toasted almonds, finely chopped	60 mL
	pinch of salt	
¼ tsp	sweet Spanish or Hungarian paprika	1 mL
⅜ cup	vegetable oil	90 mL

METHOD:

In a bowl, combine the dry ingredients, add the oil and mix until well blended, press into a well-buttered 9-in/22.5-cm pie plate. Bake at 400°F/200°C for about 10 minutes, or until golden. Cool.

DIANE'S SECRETS:

When asparagus are at their peak, I like to add a layer of blanched spears (10–12). Pour in half of the filling, spread an even layer of the asparagus spears, top with the rest of the filling and bake.

FILLING:

1 cup	**smoked salmon, leftover**	250 mL
	baked or grilled salmon	
	OR	
6 ½-oz	**can salmon**	160 g
3	**eggs, slightly beaten**	3
½ cup	**sour cream**	125 mL
½ cup	**yogurt**	125 mL
¼ cup	**mayonnaise**	60 mL
½ cup	**grated cheddar cheese**	125 mL
2 tbsp	**green onion,**	30 mL
	finely chopped	
1 tbsp	**chopped dill**	15 mL
	shot of Tabasco	

METHOD:

Slice the salmon into small cubes. If using canned salmon, drain and flake, reserving the liquid. In a bowl, blend the eggs, sour cream, yogurt and mayonnaise (plus salmon liquid if using canned). Fold in the salmon, cheese, onions, dill and Tabasco. Spoon into the shell and bake at 325°F / 160°C for about 40 minutes or until firm. Can be made a day ahead and refrigerated, or serve immediately. To reheat, bake at 325°F/160°C for about 30 minutes, or until hot.

This can be prepared on the morning of serving: Prepare the crust and filling. Set the crust aside, refrigerate the salmon filling. Just before serving, fill the baked shell with the filling and bake according to directions.

Main
Courses
Chicken

CHICKEN HAWAIIAN

Serves 12 for a buffet, 8 as a main entrée.

I think everyone who has ever taken a cooking class from me the past three decades has served this Hawaiian chicken dish. It can be done ahead of time and freezes well. Serve with **Oriental Fried Vegetable Rice** (pg. 114) or **Thai Rice with Coconut Milk** (pg. 115). It's fun for summertime entertaining.

16	**skinned, deboned free-range chicken breasts, cut in half**	16
¼ cup	white wine	60 mL

ONIONS:

2 tbsp	olive oil	30 mL
2	**medium onions, thinly sliced**	2

MARINADE:

¼ cup	soy sauce	60 mL
½ cup	**dry white wine, divided**	125 mL
	zest and juice of 1 large lime	
2	**cloves garlic, pressed**	2
2 tbsp	**peeled fresh ginger, finely chopped**	30 mL
1 tsp	**curry powder, or to taste**	5 mL
	pepper	

DIANE'S SECRETS:

I have eliminated the butter and flour from the original recipe to cut down on the fat. The results are just as delicious.

METHOD:

Blend the marinade ingredients using ¼ cup / 60 mL dry white wine. Pour over the chicken in a large bowl and marinate for 2–3 hours, turning occasionally. Remove the chicken, saving the marinade. In a non-stick pan or stove grill pan, sear the chicken breasts on both sides. Place the chicken in a single layer in a large casserole dish. Set aside.

In a skillet, heat the olive oil and sauté the sliced onions until golden and softened. Sprinkle the onion slices over the chicken, then pour over the reserved marinade. Can be made the day ahead and refrigerated, or frozen.

TO SERVE:

Bake, covered, at 350°F / 180°C oven for about 20 minutes . Uncover, pour over it the remaining ¼ cup / 60 mL dry white wine and bake for another 10 minutes, or until just cooked.

CHICKEN BREASTS SUPREME

Serves 8–10

This is another *Chef on the Run* classic recipe and one of the most popular. Some claim it's the best baked chicken they've ever eaten. Now that's a compliment! Its tangy sour cream marinade keeps the chicken moist. Any leftovers are perfect for picnics or sandwiches.

12	boned, skinned free-range chicken breasts, cut in half	12

MARINADE:

3 cups	sour cream	750 mL
	juice of 1 lemon	
½ tsp	Worcestershire sauce	2.5 mL
½ tsp	celery salt	2.5 mL
¾ tsp	sweet Spanish or Hungarian paprika	3 mL
1	large clove garlic, pressed	1
¼ tsp	salt	1 mL
	pepper to taste	

COATING:

2 ½ cups	fine dry bread crumbs	625 mL

METHOD:

On the day before serving, in a large bowl combine the marinade ingredients and blend well. Add the chicken pieces to the sour cream mixture, coating each piece well, and let stand in bowl covered overnight.

On the morning of serving, remove the chicken breasts one by one, leaving a good coating of sour cream on each, and coat well with the bread crumbs. Arrange on a shallow greased baking sheet, cover and refrigerate until ready to bake.

TO SERVE:

Bake uncovered in a preheated 350°F/180°C oven for 25–30 minutes or, just until cooked.

DIANE'S SECRETS:

Again, I have eliminated the butter and shortening mixture that topped the chicken while baking, to cut down on the fat, and the results are just as tasty. You can substitute low-fat sour cream for the regular sour cream if you wish.

KENYAN CHICKEN (KUKU) WITH CORNMEAL CAKE (UGALI)

Serves 12–16

The Vancouver Sun Run started out in 1985 with 3,000 participants. We now have more than 40,000 taking part, from the elite international athlete to the layperson jogger to the avid walker to the wheelchair wizard.

Talented Kenyan men and women have won many of our 10K runs, and Kenyans are very much part of our yearly event in Vancouver. The run is now ranked in the top 10 runs in the world! Three of the top Kenyan distance runners in the winners' circle — Evan Rutto, James Koskei and Sally Barsosyo — put on their chefs' hats and prepared their native chicken dish for several of the volunteers and athletes at a post–Sun Run party hosted by. Ken Elmer and Jan Neufeld, who were in their kitchen surpervising as I took notes on this unique Kenyan dish.

Chicken, or "kuku," is served with a white cornmeal dish known as "ugali." This white cornmeal can be found in specialty stores and is the same as the cornmeal that is used in Southern cooking in the United States. The kitchen was full of excited tasters watching the Kenyan trio preparing the dish as fast as they run! It's simple in its ingredients, very healthy to eat and part of the basic daily diet in Kenya. We were not disappointed: it was enjoyed by all!

2 tbsp	olive oil	30 mL
3	onions, chopped	3
1	large red pepper, coarsely chopped	1
8	chicken legs plus 8 chicken thighs, chopped into bite-size pieces	8
4	bunches fresh kale ("sukuma" in Kenya), coarsely chopped, about 16 cups/4 L	4
5	large tomatoes, coarsely chopped, about 2 cups/500 mL	5
1 tbsp	salt	15 mL
½ cup	chopped parsley	125 mL

METHOD:

In a large Dutch oven or other stock pot, heat the olive oil. Sauté the onions and pepper until slightly soft and golden. Add the chicken pieces and simmer for 5–10 minutes, stirring constantly.

Add the kale, tomatoes and salt. Cover the pot and simmer at medium heat for 25–30 minutes, or until the chicken is tender and there are no pink juices. Stir the chicken dish from time to time while it is simmering; you may have to turn the heat down if too hot. Add the chopped parsley and serve with Cornmeal Cake.

CORNMEAL CAKE (UGALI)

Serves 12–16

12 cups	**water**	3 L
6 cups	**white cornmeal**	1.5 L
2 tsp	**salt**	10 mL

GARNISH:

¼ cup	**parsley, finely chopped**	60 mL

METHOD:

In a large stock pot with a heavy bottom, bring the water to a rapid boil. Whisk in the cornmeal and blend well, stirring constantly. Add the salt. Turn the heat down and simmer uncovered, stirring from time to time with a heavy spoon, as it will thicken, for 15–20 minutes. When it starts coming away from the pot, pour or spoon onto a large platter or into a large bowl or cassrole, making a mound. Sprinkle with chopped parsley and serve with the chicken.

JUST THE FACTS — "CHICKEN GOES WITH EVERYTHING"!

Did you know that chicken is one of the most widely used meats in the world? It's so versatile and complements any type of cuisine. It's also one of the most serious of "food safe" concerns. When purchasing chicken, go to a reliable butcher or market. Always check the expiry dates on the packages. I prefer the free-range or run-free chickens, or organic. Always store fresh, uncooked chicken in the coldest part of the refrigerator for no more than two days. Never thaw fowl, meat or fish on the counter. Always use a separate chopping board. Have a few heavy plastic chopping sheets to put on top of your counter or wooden chopping board to prevent contamination. In checking the doneness of chicken, pierce into the middle, and if the juices are clear and the meat thermometer reads 165°F / 75°C, it's ready to serve.

TUSCAN CHICKEN
WITH ORZO

Serves 8

I rely on this Tuscan dish for informal entertaining when I'm on the go. Both the chicken and the orzo can be prepared ahead of time. I pick up several antipasto items from my favourite deli, along with rustic breads, biscottis and two or three sorbets. With very little effort we are ready to dine and wine. Don't forget to pick up a few robust Italian wines!

8	single free-range chicken breasts, boned, skinned, cut in half	8
5 tbsp	olive oil	75 mL
2	onions, finely chopped	2
1 cup	sun-dried tomatoes in oil, drained well, julienned	250 mL
1/3 cup	balsamic vinegar	80 mL
1 1/2 cups	dry white wine	375 mL
	salt and pepper to taste	
1 cup	fresh basil leaves, julienned	250 mL
	additional basil strips for garnish	

METHOD:

In a large sauté pan, heat 3 tbsp/45 mL of the oil. Sauté the chicken breasts, a few at a time, for about 3 minutes on each side until just opaque, with no pink juices. Place in a large, shallow casserole. Refrigerate while you prepare the onions.

Add remaining 2 tbsp/30 mL oil to the chicken pan. Add the onions, sauté until slightly caramelized and deep golden, 5–8 minutes. Add the sun-dried tomatoes, balsamic vinegar, wine and pepper. Simmer for about 10 minutes to reduce the sauce and thicken slightly. Add the fresh basil and pour evenly over the chicken. Can be refrigerated at this stage a day ahead, or in the morning, and baked just before serving.

TO SERVE:

Bake at 350°F/180°C oven for about 30 minutes, or until the chicken is heated through. Sprinkle additional basil on top and serve with **Orzo with Parmesan Cheese** (pg. 116) or other pasta.

BASIL ROASTED CHICKEN
WITH GARLIC SAUCE

Serves 6–8

Yes, there are 40 cloves of garlic in this recipe. Garlic sweetens as it roasts, and when puréed becomes a perfect creamy base for the sauce. Even the non-garlic fans admitted they were pleasantly surprised by how mellow and tasty it was. Serve with mashed potatoes or **Potatoes Gratin** (pg. 123) and **Roasted Vegetables** (pg. 126).

2	**3 1/2 lb / 1.6 kg free-range chickens, cleaned (run finger under skin to loosen)**	2
	salt and pepper to taste	
3 tbsp	**dried basil**	45 mL
1 cup	**fresh basil**	250 mL
½ cup	**dry white wine**	125 mL
40	**large cloves garlic, peeled**	40
1 cup	**chicken stock**	250 mL
1 cup	**fresh basil, julienned**	250 mL

METHOD:

Remove the giblets and neck from the chickens. Rinse well and pat dry. Sprinkle inside and out with salt and pepper.

Put half of the dried basil under the skin of each chicken. Rub the remaining basil over the top. Season with salt and pepper. Place breast side up in a roasting pan. Roast for 30 minutes at 400°F / 200°C, then reduce heat to 350°F/180°C. Add the garlic and baste both the garlic and chicken with the pan juices. Roast for 15 minutes more, pour the wine over the chicken, and roast for another 60–70 minutes, or until temperature reaches 165°F/75°C (use a meat thermometer) and the legs are soft, with no pink juices. Remove the chicken and pour the pan juices and garlic into a food processor. Add 1 cup/250 mL chicken stock, purée and strain, pressing the garlic with the back of a spoon, into a saucepan. Simmer for about 10 minutes to thicken slightly. Add the fresh basil and more pepper to taste. You may want to add chicken stock and a little wine to give you more sauce.

ROASTED CHICKEN
WITH **PASTA STUFFING**

Serves 4

Have you ever stuffed a chicken with *"pasta"*? When I read the recipe in the fabulous Australian magazine *Vogue Entertaining and Travel* I was curious to try it. This is my version of the unique and totally fun idea of stuffing your chicken with creamy pasta. Start the dinner off with an antipasto platter and a robust Italian wine. For the fun of it, slice the stuffed bird at the table. Add a side dish of roasted julienned strips of pepper and fresh asparagus. Citrus sorbets and Italian macaroons make a perfect finale.

PASTA STUFFING:

2 cups	dried gnocchi pasta noodles (medium shells)	500 mL
2 tbsp	olive oil	30 mL
2	cloves garlic, finely chopped	2
2 cups	stemmed mushrooms, coarsely chopped	500 mL
1	onion, finely chopped (about 1 cup / 250 mL)	1
½ cup	Parmesan cheese	125 mL
½ cup	chèvre, cut into small cubes	125 mL
1 cup	cream	250 mL
½ cup	whole milk	125 mL
2 tbsp	fresh basil	30 mL
	salt and pepper to taste	
1 ½ cups	chicken stock	375 mL
1 cup	additional grated Parmesan cheese	250 mL

METHOD:

Cook the pasta noodles according to directions, for about 10 minutes, or until *al dente*. Don't overcook. While the pasta is cooking, heat the olive oil in a sauté pan. Add the garlic, mushrooms and onion, a little salt and pepper. Sauté for a few minutes, until softened. Set aside. When the pasta is ready, drain and put into a large bowl. Add the mushroom mixture, ½ cup/125 mL Parmesan cheese and toss. In a separate bowl, with a whisk, blend the chèvre and cream until smooth. Add to the pasta mixture along with the basil, blending well. Salt and pepper to taste. Refrigerate while you prepare the chicken.

CHICKEN:

2 ½ –3 lb	**free-range chicken**	1–1.5 kg
	olive oil	
	salt and pepper to taste	

GARNISH:

2	**roasted red peppers, thinly sliced**	2

METHOD:

Set the oven to 450°F/230°C. Rinse the chicken inside and out, pat dry. Put into a shallow casserole or small roasting pan. Rub a little olive oil over the bird and sprinkle with salt and pepper. Refrigerate while you prepare the pasta stuffing. When ready, stuff the cavity and neck of the chicken with the stuffing. Close the cavity and neck with small poultry pins, tie the legs with oven string. Pour the chicken stock over the bird and roast at 450°F/230°C until meat temperature reaches 165°F/75°C, or until legs are soft and there are no pink juices, about 1 ½ hours. Baste the bird frequently with the chicken stock.

TO SERVE:

Slice the chicken, serve with the pasta stuffing, juices, roasted peppers and asparagus. Pass the remaining grated Parmesan cheese.

DIANE'S SECRETS:

You can prepare the pasta stuffing on the morning of serving and refrigerate. Just before roasting, stuff the bird. You may have a little stuffing left over; it can be put in a separate small casserole, covered with tinfoil and baked during the last half hour of roasting the bird.

I like to roast this dish at a higher temperature, 450°F/230°C, to take less time. This method produces a crispy skin and moist chicken. The creamy juices from the stuffing overflow into the chicken stock, which gives you a fabulous sauce for the chicken and pasta stuffing.

The Italian gnocchi pasta noodles made with durum semolina are used in this recipe, *not* the Italian potato-based gnocchi. This pasta is found in most Italian specialty sections of your grocery or deli.

HOW TO COOK PASTA:

Use a large, deep pot that can hold about 6 qt / 6L of water for each pound of pasta. The more water you use, the less gummy the cooked pasta will be. Bring the water to a hard, rolling boil, add 1–2 tbsp / 15-30 mL oil, then add the pasta in small batches, stirring after each addition with a large wooden fork, gently separating the strands. When all pasta is added, make sure it is submerged in the water to cook evenly. Some Italian chefs say, "NEVER put oil in the pasta water," while others swear by it. Your call! Drain immediately when cooked. You may wish to keep some of the pasta stock in case you want to thin your sauce. Do not rinse the pasta, unless it's to be used in a cold salad or tossed in an oil marinade. Rinsing in cold water will remove the starches, which prevents the sauce from clinging to the pasta.

ANNETTE'S MOROCCAN
ROASTED CHICKEN

Serves 12–15

Annette Kingery has been developing Moroccan recipes for years in her Las Vegas kitchen. Like all good cooks, she doesn't need a recipe: she cooks by taste and from the heart. She shared some of her specialty dishes with us, and the Moroccan chicken was especially superb. Start off this exotic dinner with **Turkish Meze** (pg. 46).

16	**single free-range chicken**	16
	breasts, boned, skinned, cut in half	
6	**medium onions, thinly sliced**	6
1 cup	**water**	250 mL
¼ cup	**vegetable oil**	60 mL
¼ tsp	**dried saffron threads**	1 mL
	dissolved in 1/4 cup / 60 mL water	
1 tsp	**pepper**	5 mL
	salt to taste	
4 tsp	**cinnamon**	20 mL
1 cup	**raisins or currants**	250 mL
1 cup	**blanched almonds**	250 mL

METHOD:

Cook onions, uncovered, in 1 cup / 250 mL water over medium heat until water is absorbed and onions soft. In a skillet, heat the vegetable oil, add the soft onions and sauté until golden. Set aside.

Place chicken breasts in a large bowl. Add the saffron, salt, pepper, 2 tsp / 10 mL cinnamon and sautéed onions, mix well. Put in a single layer in a large roasting pan. Cover and bake at 400°F/200°C for about 12 minutes; uncover and bake for a further 12 minutes. Add raisins, sprinkle with the remaining cinnamon. Bake for a further 10–15 minutes, or until golden brown. Cool and refrigerate.

Just before serving, add the almonds to the casserole. Reheat, uncovered, in a 350°F/180°C oven for about 35 minutes, or until hot. If chicken starts to dry out, sprinkle with a little chicken stock and cover pan with foil. If necessary, brown finished dish under broiler.

DAVID'S CHICKEN AND ARTICHOKES IN PHYLLO PAPER

Serves 6

This Greek pie is my twin brother David's favourite. First served to Doug and me in Toronto by my sister-in-law, Dianne Matheson, this tasty pie has been a big hit with my family ever since, and with my cooking class students. It looks as good as it tastes! I usually make two pies while I'm at it: it's no more effort than making one, and the second pie goes into the freezer for emergencies. Serve with a mango chutney and thin slices of red and yellow peppers sautéed in a little olive oil and a pinch of red pepper flakes. Don't be afraid to tackle phyllo paper — it's easy! Just follow the recipe.

6	boneless, skinless free-range chicken breasts	6
	zest and juice of 1 lemon	
3	6 1/2 oz / 160 g jars of marinated artichoke hearts, drained	3
3 tbsp	chopped dill	45 mL
½ cup	green onions, finely chopped	125 mL
	salt and pepper to taste	

SAUCE:

1½ cups	whole milk	375 mL
	zest of 1 lemon	
¼ cup	chicken stock	60 mL
3 tbsp	butter	45 mL
¼ cup	flour	60 mL
	salt and pepper to taste	

METHOD:

A day ahead of serving, cook the chicken breasts by covering with foil and baking in a 350°F/180°C degree oven for 30–35 minutes, or until tender and opaque. Don't let them dry out. Cube the meat into 1-in/2.5-cm chunks. Put into a large bowl, sprinkle with lemon juice, saving the zest for the sauce. Add the artichoke hearts, dill and onions; add salt and pepper to taste; toss to blend. Refrigerate.

In a small saucepan on medium heat, warm the milk, zest of lemon and chicken stock, or microwave in a bowl for 1½ minutes.

In a separate saucepan, melt the butter and blend in the flour. Add the milk mixture slowly and bring to a gentle boil. Drop to medium heat, stirring constantly until thickened. Add salt and pepper to taste. Cool. Fold the sauce into the chicken and artichoke mixture, blending well. Refrigerate until cooled, about 20 minutes.

PIE:

10	**sheets of phyllo paper**	10
½ cup	**butter**	125 mL

METHOD:

Melt the butter in a small saucepan; keep on low while you prepare the phyllo paper shell.

Lightly butter both sides of 10 sheets of phyllo paper as you go along (I use my hands for this). Drape one on the left side and another on the right side of a 10-in/25-cm springform pan, overlapping the sheets slightly in the middle. Spoon in the chicken mixture and pat down evenly. Bring the phyllo paper sheets into the middle to cover the chicken; twist them together to form a small flower. Brush with a little more butter. Bake at 375°F/190°C for about 40 minutes, or until golden.

To reheat the next day, bake at 375°F/190°C for 30–35 minutes, or until heated through. Cover with tinfoil for the first 20 minutes, then uncover for the remaining time to crisp the phyllo. Watch that it doesn't overbrown.

DIANE'S SECRETS:

To prevent the central flower from becoming too brown, cover it with foil once it has turned golden.

If you plan to freeze the pie, bake it for 30 minutes, or until the pastry is crisp and golden. Remove from oven and cool. Freezer wrap and freeze.

To thaw: Frozen pies should be thawed overnight in the refrigerator. Reheat, covered, at 375°F/190°C for about 30 minutes, or until hot. Cover with tinfoil for the first 20 minutes to prevent overbrowning the phyllo paper. Remove the foil for the remaining 10 minutes to crisp the phyllo.

CAL-MEX CHICKEN FIESTA

Serves 6

This entertaining idea comes from former Canadian Olympic 3,000-metre bronze-medallist runner Lynn Williams, who acquired a taste for California-style Mexican cuisine while training in San Diego. With four active children and as co-owner of specialty running stores in the Lower Mainland, Lynn is truly "on the run"! Her casual Cal-Mex Chicken Fiesta menu makes it easy for her to entertain. Everyone creates an individual version of the traditional fajitas. Make sure to have lots of well-chilled Mexican Corona beer on hand!

VEGETABLES:

1	green onion, finely chopped	1
1 inch	fresh ginger, peeled, finely chopped	2.5 cm
1	clove garlic, finely chopped	1
2	green peppers, thinly sliced	2
2	red peppers, thinly sliced	2
1	large onion, thinly sliced	1

METHOD:

Combine all in a bowl. Set aside.

MARINADE FOR CHICKEN AND BEEF:

½	onion, chopped	½
1	clove garlic, pressed	1
1 tsp	peeled fresh ginger, finely chopped	5 mL
¼ cup	water	60 mL
1 ½ tsp	brown sugar	7.5 mL
1 ½ cups	soy sauce	375 mL
½ cup	water	125 mL

METHOD:

Place first four marinade ingredients in food processor or blender and blend well. Add rest of marinade ingredients. Put the chicken and beef strips in separate bowls. Pour the marinade equally over each, leave to marinate for an hour or more. Drain each well, saving the marinade.

To sauté chicken, heat 2 tbsp/30 mL vegetable oil in a skillet or wok. Add the chicken and stir-fry until cooked. Remove to an ovenproof dish.

CHICKEN AND BEEF:

1 lb	**chicken breast, deboned, skin removed and cut into 2-in/5-cm strips**	450 g
1 lb	**Flank or rump steak, sliced across the grain in 2-in/5-cm strips**	450 g
12	**10-in/25-cm flour tortillas**	12

METHOD:

To sauté beef, heat 2 tbsp/30 mL vegetable oil in a skillet or wok. Add the beef and stir-fry until cooked. Remove to an ovenproof dish, separate from the chicken.

When the chicken and beef are cooked, cover each with equal amounts of the vegetable mixture. Pour 1/4 cup/60 mL of the reserved marinade over each and sprinkle 1 tbsp/15 mL of oil over each. Refrigerate until ready to serve.

TO SERVE:

Just before serving, place chicken and beef dishes under broiler and broil until sizzling. Serve while still sizzling. Guests use the meats and vegetables to stuff their own tortillas. Serve the tortillas warm: wrap them in a damp kitchen towel and place in warm oven for about 30 minutes.

Serve with Mexican condiments: salsa, chopped green onions, grated Monterey Jack and cheddar cheeses, chopped tomatoes and so on. To round out the meal, add **Williams' Mexican Rice** (pg. 130) and refried beans.

MEXICAN TORTA (CHILAQUILES)

Makes 4 tortas, serves 8–10 as an appetizer, serves 4 as a main entrée

Tortillas are stacked with various fillings, then baked until golden and crisp. Let everyone create their own chilaquile! Pick up most of the ingredients from your Mexican specialty deli for an easy, informal and fun dinner party. They are equally popular as appetizers.

12	8-in / 20-cm flour tortillas	12
1 cup	enchilada sauce	250 mL
2	cooked chicken breasts, thinly sliced	2
2 cups	grated sharp cheddar cheese	500 mL
2 cups	grated Monterey Jack cheese	500 mL
½ cup	green onions, finely chopped	125 mL
2	jalapeno peppers, seeded, finely chopped, or 1 small can chopped green chilies	2
15 oz	can refried black beans	375 g
	vegetable oil	

METHOD:

Assemble the 4 tortas an hour or so before serving. Refrigerate until ready to bake.

To make flour tortillas, heat about 2 tbsp / 30 mL oil in a skillet on medium heat. Fry one tortilla at a time until lightly browned and crisp, about 10 seconds on each side. Add a little more oil each time if needed. Pat dry on paper towels.

To assemble, use 2 cookie sheets and build 2 tortas on each. On each cookie sheet, start with 2 tortillas, side by side. Spread a thin layer of the enchilada sauce on each. Top with the chicken slices, sprinkle a little of the cheddar and Monterey Jack cheeses over the chicken, than a little of the green onions and the jalapeno peppers.

Top with the second tortilla. Spread a little of the enchilada sauce on the tortilla. Spread a layer of the refried beans followed by the rest of the cheeses. Sprinkle the rest of the onions and chilies on top of the cheese. Top with the third tortilla. Press down slightly. Refrigerate until ready to bake.

To bake, heat the oven to 400°F/200°C. Cover each tortilla stack with tinfoil. Bake for 15 minutes, then remove the tinfoil and bake for 10–15 minutes more, or until the tortilla stacks are hot and slightly crispy. Watch that they don't brown.

TO SERVE:

Cut into wedges. Serve with the condiments.

GARNISH:

chopped cilantro

CONDIMENTS:

salsa, guacamole, sour cream, corn chips

Main Courses
Meats

LAMB SHANKS
WITH **ORZO**

Serves 8

This Italian dish is based on the classic Osso Buco but uses lamb shanks instead of veal and adds orzo to make a complete meal in one dish. This is total comfort food, ideal for après-ski dining. It's at its best if made a day or two ahead and reheated just before serving. Start with an Italian antipasto course, lots of hearty bread, Italian wines, **Ice Cream with Espresso and Frangelico** (pg. 214) and biscotti for the grand finale!

8	**small lamb shanks**	8
	(about 1/2 lb / 225 g each	
¼ cup + 1 tbsp	**olive oil**	60 + 15 mL
4	**large cloves garlic, finely chopped**	4
2	**carrots, finely chopped**	2
1	**large onion, chopped**	1
28 oz	**can diced tomatoes, undrained, chopped**	700 g
1 cup	**dry white wine**	250 mL
3 tbsp	**each fresh chopped oregano, thyme**	45 mL
	salt and pepper to taste	
2 ½ cups	**chicken stock**	625 mL
1 cup	**uncooked orzo**	250 mL
½ cup	**toasted pine nuts**	125 mL
1 cup	**grated Parmesan cheese**	250 mL

METHOD:

Remove skin and fat from the lamb shanks. Heat the ¼ cup / 60 mL olive oil in a large Dutch oven, sauté shanks in oil until golden. Take out and set aside.

Remove the oil. Add the 1 tbsp / 15 mL olive oil to the Dutch oven. Add garlic, carrots and onion to the pan, sauté at low heat until soft. Put the shanks back in, along with the tomatoes, wine, herbs and seasonings. Cook, uncovered, in a 350°F / 180°C oven for about 2 hours.

Take out the lamb shanks and set aside on a plate. Add chicken stock and orzo to the tomato sauce. Bring to a boil on top of the stove. Place the lamb shanks across the top of the orzo mixture.

Cover with tinfoil. Put back into the oven and continue to cook, covered, for about 20 minutes; stir to blend the pasta and sauce. Cover again for another 5–10 minutes, or until the orzo is soft (al dente) and most of the liquid has been absorbed. There will be some liquid left, but it will thicken as it cools. Cool, then refrigerate.

TO SERVE:

If the orzo mixture seems too thick, add a little chicken stock. You want a creamy texture. Reheat in covered casserole at 350°F / 180°C for 40–45 minutes or until hot.

On each serving bowl, put a good ladle of the orzo, set a lamb shank in the middle of the pasta, sprinkle with a few pine nuts and a little Parmesan cheese. Serve. Pass extra Parmesan.

DIANE'S SECRETS:

This dish freezes well. Thaw overnight in the refrigerator, reheat at 350°F / 180°C for about 40 minutes, or until hot.

BARBECUED BUTTERFLIED
LEG OF LAMB

Serves 8–10

One of the easiest and tastiest ways of serving lamb! Marinate the lamb in a mixture of herbs and wine for several hours, then put on to the coals. **Potatoes Gratin** (pg. 123), **Ruth's Baked Spanish Onions** (pg. 125) and **Roasted Vegetables** (pg. 126) are my choice to accompany the lamb.

1	whole leg of lamb, boned	1
¼ cup	olive oil	60 mL
MARINADE:		
1 tsp	dried basil	5 mL
1 tsp	dried marjoram	5 mL
1 tsp	dried rosemary	5 mL
1 tsp	salt	5 mL
1 tsp	pepper	5 mL
½ cup	dry white wine	125 mL
¼ cup	Worcestershire sauce	60 mL

METHOD:

Have your butcher bone and "butterfly" the lamb. Hammer the surface with a meat cleaver. In a bowl, whisk the marinade ingredients to blend well. Put the lamb into a large, strong plastic bag, pour in the marinade to coat all over. Tie the meat up tightly inside the bag, so the meat keeps moist all over. Refrigerate for 6–12 hours.

To barbecue, brush the lamb all over with the olive oil and place over the coals, but don't put it too close to them. Grill about 6 inches / 15 cm above the flames. Allow about 20 minutes per side, until the outside is crusty brown and inside a tender pink. Brush the lamb frequently with the marinade as it cooks. When ready, slice thinly.

DIANE'S SECRETS:

When cooking under an oven grill, place lamb in a shallow pan and grill as directed here.

ROSEMARY

One of my favourites, rosemary is the king of the aromatic herbs! Its rich flavour enhances roasted vegetables and meats, particularly lamb. It's great for garnishing dinner plates and is at its best when fresh.

MEDITERRANEAN
RACK OF LAMB

Serves 4

As you have gathered, Doug and I enjoy lamb! Try this Mediterranean Rub on your next rack-of-lamb dinner; it's a tasty alternative to the usual bread crumb coating. Serve with **Potatoes Gratin** (pg. 123), **Roasted Vegetables** (pg. 126) or fresh asparagus.

3	racks of lamb, French-cut (trimmed of fat), allowing 3 loins per person and leftovers	3

MEDITERRANEAN RUB:

½ cup	parsley, chopped	125 mL
½ cup	pitted Kalamata olives	125 mL
½ cup	sun-dried tomatoes, chopped	125 mL
1 tbsp	grainy mustard	5 mL
1	large egg, beaten	1

METHOD:

The day ahead of serving, in a food processor combine the Mediterranean Rub ingredients until slightly chunky. Put in a sealed container and refrigerate. On the morning of serving, dip the racks in the beaten egg. Pat the Mediterranean Rub evenly over the 3 racks of lamb. Refrigerate.

Take out of the fridge about 30 minutes before roasting. Put in a roasting pan and cook for about 30 minutes at 400°F/200°C for medium doneness.

TO SERVE:

Slice each rack into loins.

DIANE'S SECRETS:

Order your racks of lamb a few days before serving. I allow an extra rack for seconds, or for "leftovers" the next day!

PORK TENDERLOIN SUPERB

Serves 8

A last-minute lifesaver, this easy but impressive pork dish goes back to the first cooking class I gave, more than 20 years ago. This is my new version of this dish, inspired by our visit to China. I dedicate it to all my students who gave me the inspiration to publish *The Chef on The Run* series! Serve this with **Oriental Fried Vegetable Rice** (pg. 114), or **Thai Rice** (pg. 115) with **Singaporean Spicy Asparagus with Shiitake Mushroom Sauce** (pg. 131).

3	pork tenderloins	3
	(about 1 lb /450 g each)	

MARINADE:

½ cup	soy sauce	125 mL
½ cup	rye whisky or Scotch	125 mL
¼ cup	brown sugar	60 mL

PORK RUB:

⅓ cup	fresh peeled ginger, finely chopped	80 mL
2 tbsp	soy sauce	30 mL
3	cloves garlic, finely chopped	3
½ tsp	Chinese 5-spice powder	125 mL
	pepper to taste	
	toasted sesame seeds	

METHOD:

Trim and clean tenderloins and marinate for 2–3 hours. Meanwhile, in a small bowl, combine the pork-rub ingredients. Set aside. After 2–3 hours drain the marinade off the tenderloins, reserving the marinade. Put the tenderloins in a roasting pan. Pat the pork-rub mixture evenly on both sides of the tenderloins, sprinkle each side with the sesame seeds. Can be refrigerated until ready to roast.

TO SERVE:

Roast in a preheated 375°F / 190°C oven for 35–40 minutes, or until there are no pink juices remaining. Baste the tenderloins with the reserved marinade from time to time.

Slice thinly on the diagonal and drizzle any remaining meat juices over the slices before serving.

DIANE'S SECRETS:

The 5-spice powder used in Chinese cooking is a blend of fennel, star anise, cassia bark, Sichuan pepper and cloves. It can be purchased in any Chinese specialty food section at markets.

FRENCH CANADIAN TOURTIÈRE WITH SOUR CREAM SAUCE

Serves 6–8

Over the decades it has become a family tradition to serve my version of the French Canadian tourtière during the Christmas holiday season. This delectable adaptation of the classic Quebec tourtière can be baked and frozen weeks ahead of serving. Thaw overnight in the refrigerator and bake as directed.

PASTRY:

2 ½ cups	flour	625 mL
½ tsp	salt	2 mL
12 tbsp	chilled butter	180 mL
1	large egg	1
½ cup	sour cream	125 mL

FILLING:

3 tbsp	butter	45 mL
½	onion, finely chopped	½
1 cup	chopped mushrooms	250 mL
2 lb	lean ground meat	1 kg
	(combination of beef, pork and veal)	
¼ cup	parsley, finely chopped	60 mL
	salt and pepper to taste	
⅛ tsp	savory	.5 mL
⅛ tsp	ground cloves	.5 mL
¼ tsp	celery salt	1 mL
½ cup	milk	125 mL
1	egg, slightly beaten	1
1 cup	sharp cheddar cheese, grated	250 mL
½ cup	bread crumbs	125 mL

METHOD:

In a food processor, blend the flour and salt. Add small pieces of butter and blend just until it flakes. In a bowl, mix egg and sour cream and add to the flour mixture. Blend just enough to form into a ball. Don't overmix! Wrap in wax paper and store in refrigerator. Can be made 2 days ahead of making the pie, or frozen for future use.

METHOD:

Melt the butter in a large skillet. Sauté the onion and mushrooms until tender. Set aside. Add the meat to the skillet and sauté until browned. Remove excess fat, leaving only 1 tbsp. Return onion and mushrooms to the pan and add seasonings, milk, bread crumbs, egg and cheese. Simmer over low heat for about 3 minutes. Refrigerate for about 20 minutes, or until cold.

DECADENT GRAPES IN WHITE CHOCOLATE:

Serves 4–6

These are always a big hit for special occasions. Serve with any dessert, especially with ice creams and sorbets, but they are also delectable on their own. The grapes have to be perfectly crisp, and use only the best-quality white chocolate.

1	bunch green seeded grapes, making about 20 clusters	1
8 oz	white chocolate	200 g

METHOD:

A day ahead, cut off small bunches of washed and dried grapes and dip into melted chocolate, turning to coat each grape well. Place on a cookie sheet lined with parchment paper. Refrigerate.

DIANE'S SECRETS:

You have to watch the temperature when you are melting the chocolate, or it will "cease" or separate. In the microwave, start melting for about 1 ½ minutes at a time, but check after 1 minute. On the stove, melt in a double boiler.

DONNA'S KILLER BROWNIES

During a 50-day trip in the fall of 2001 we had 35 days aboard the cruise ship *Regal Princess*, where we met passengers from all over the world. Sharing our dining-room table with us from Bangkok to Sydney were a dynamic couple from San Francisco, Donna and Dave Manahan. While I was busy working away on my laptop, finishing this book, Donna was busy making beautiful teddy bears to donate to auctions for their local charities. Donna also is an avid cook and they enjoy entertaining at home. She told us about her "Killer Brownies" and sent me her recipe to include in *Chef on the Run*. Let me tell you, these are unbelievable! You, too, will become "famous" once you serve these brownies. But remember, good things come in small packages! Use self-control. It's a special treat — slice in mini squares.

1	package Betty Crocker Supermoist German Chocolate Cake Mix	1
1	large egg	1
1 cup	butter, divided	250 mL
½ cup	evaporated milk	125 mL
14 oz	bag Kraft caramels (or comparable brand)	350 g
1 cup	chopped walnuts	250 mL
1	12-oz / 300-g bag chocolate chips	1

METHOD:

Mix together cake mix, egg and ½ cup /125 mL butter. Set aside 1 ½ cups / 375 mL of this mixture. Press the remaining amount into a well-greased 9½ × 13-in /23.75 × 32.5-cm baking dish or pan. It will be very dry, but spread it out as well as possible and it will rise to form a solid first layer. Bake at 350°F/180°C for 10–12 minutes, or until dry. Cool for 10 minutes.

Place caramels and remaining ½ cup/125 mL butter, covered, in microwave for 2 minutes, remove and whisk together, then return for an additional minute and whisk again. Stir in the milk until smooth, using a hand or regular mixer; blend for 1–2 minutes until very creamy. Pour over the brownies.

Mix together by hand the reserved cake mixture from step 1, the chocolate chips and nuts. Crumble over the caramel layer and bake at 350°F/180°C for 25–30 minutes. Cool on a rack for 1 hour, then refrigerate an hour before cutting. Keep covered in the refrigerator until ready to use, or seal well and freeze . Will keep for months. To serve, thaw and keep in the refrigerator.

DIANE'S SECRETS:

Donna's comments: "These take time to make, but it is more than well worth the effort. People just go crazy for them. It has become a ritual that Dave takes the cellophane wrappers off the caramels for me while watching a football game or movie. I usually make 2 or 3 batches at a time to dole out with my Christmas cookies every year."

JEN AND VINCENT'S LEMON CAKE
WITH SEASONAL BERRIES

Makes 10–12 thin wedges

Our daughter Jennifer and her husband Vincent love anything lemon as much as I do. When I served this latest "lemon" creation for the first time at one of our family dinners, they declared this cake the "ultimate"! If I had to choose the perfect marriage for summer berries, this is it! The lemon pound cake is quick to whip up, smooth as silk and oh, so lemony! I must confess that it does have one pint of whipping cream in the batter — but no butter. Serve in thin wedges. And remember, it's for a special treat! Serve with fresh summer berries and a scoop of lemon sorbet, naturally.

5	large eggs	5	METHOD:
2 cups	sugar	500 mL	In a large bowl, beat the eggs with an electric mixer
3 cups	flour	750 mL	until thick and pale yellow. Gradually beat in the
4 tsp	baking powder	20 mL	sugar.
	pinch of salt		
	zest of 3 large lemons, finely chopped		Mix the flour with the baking powder, salt and
1 tbsp	vanilla extract	15 mL	lemon zest. Set aside.
2 cups	whipping cream	500 mL	

In a separate bowl, blend the vanilla with the whipping cream. Alternately add the flour and cream to the eggs, beginning and ending with the flour. Pour the batter into a greased and floured 9-in/22.5-cm springform pan. Bake at 325°F/160°C for about 1½ hours, or until the cake feels firm to touch and a cake tester inserted in the centre comes out clean.

GLAZE:

In a small bowl, blend the lemon juice and sugar. Poke tiny holes all over the top of the cake, spoon lemon mixture evenly on top of the warm cake to let it soak in. Cool cake in its pan on a rack. Can be made a day ahead: Wrap well and keep at room temperature. This cake also freezes well.

GLAZE:

	juice of 3 lemons	
	(about 1/2 cup/125 mL)	
⅓ cup	sugar	80 mL

AILEEN'S GLORIOUS PEACH PIE

Serves 6

Aileen Dawson, my sister-in-law Dianne Matheson's mother, is the *grande dame* at making the best pies anyone has ever had the joy of eating! Aileen has been spoiling her family with pies for more than six decades and she has the magic touch. There is nothing like a simple fresh fruit pie just out of the oven, oozing with flavour, with pastry that melts in your mouth. "I wish," you say. "My pies are always a disaster!" Well, no more! Whenever Doug and I are in Toronto when the peaches are at their peak, Dianne knows we will wait with great anticipation after dinner for her to present Aileen's peach pie — *à la mode*, of course!

PASTRY SHELL:

Aileen swears by the original Tenderflake recipe for pastry and makes enough for several pies, depending on whether they have single or double crusts. Freeze whatever is left over for future pies.

6 cups	pastry flour	1.5 L
	OR	
5 ½ cups	all-purpose flour	1.4 L
2 tsp	salt	30 mL
1	small box Tenderflake lard	1
1 tbsp	white vinegar	15 mL
+ 1 egg in a 1-cup / 250-mL measure		
(add water to make up to 1 cup / 250 mL)		

METHOD:

Preheat oven to 375°F/190°C. Put the flour in a mixing bowl. Add the soft lard in small pieces. With a pastry blender, work the lard into the flour until it is the size of peas. Make a well in the centre, add the liquid, mix well. Knead for a few minutes to form a smooth dough. Slice off enough of the dough for a single crust, refrigerate for about 30 minutes before rolling out. Cut the rest of the pastry for single or double crusts, wrap well and freeze.

Roll out the remaining pastry thinly to line a 9- or 10-in/22.5- or 25-cm pie plate, pinching around the top. Refrigerate.

FILLING:

5	**ripe peaches, peeled, cut into thin slices**	5
¼ cup	**fresh blueberries (optional)**	60 mL
⅓ cup	**sliced almonds (optional)**	80 mL
1 cup	**white sugar**	250 mL
2	**eggs**	2
2 tbsp	**flour**	30 mL
1 ½–2 tbsp	**melted butter**	7.5–10 mL
1 tsp	**almond flavouring**	5 mL

METHOD:

Arrange the peach slices in the pastry shell by overlapping in a circular pattern. Arrange the blueberries, if desired, in the centre of the shell.

In a bowl, mix together the sugar, eggs, 2 tbsp / 30 mL flour, butter and flavouring. Pour over the peaches. Sprinkle the almonds over the peaches. Bake at 375°F/190°C for 10 minutes, then reduce the heat to 350°F/180°C and bake for another 25–30 minutes until golden on top, the filling is set and the bottom pastry is cooked.

PAPER BAG **APPLE PIE**

Serves 6

Almost everyone loves apple pie! Why not try baking your next one in a paper bag? One of my students attempted this, but put the bag too close to the hot coils. She opened the oven door and her kitchen was full of smoke. After a frantic call to the fire department she realized what she had done — the rule for baking this pie is to put it on a rack in the middle of the oven, several inches from the elements, and to have your paper bag very wet. I might add that she has baked many more Paper Bag Apple Pies over the years without requiring the assistance of the fire department!

1	**9-in /22.5-cm pie shell, unbaked**	1

FILLING:

8–10 cups	**tart apples, eg.**	2–2.5 L
	Granny Smith, cut into chunks	
½ cup	**white sugar**	125 mL
2 tbsp	**flour**	30 mL
½ tsp	**cinnamon**	2.5 mL
¼ tsp	**nutmeg**	1 mL
	juice of ½ lemon	

TOPPING:

½ cup	**sugar**	125 mL
½ cup	**flour**	125 mL
½ cup	**butter**	125 mL

METHOD:

Pare, core and quarter the apples, then halve each quarter crosswise to make large chunks. Combine ½ cup /125 mL sugar with 2 tbsp / 30 mL flour, cinnamon and nutmeg and sprinkle over the apples, tossing well to coat. Place in the unbaked pie shell and sprinkle with lemon juice.

TOPPING:

Combine the sugar, flour and butter and sprinkle over the apples to cover. Take a large brown paper grocery bag and wet it thoroughly with water. Place it on a cookie sheet and put the apple pie inside, leaving lots of room between the top of the pie and the bag for the steam to rise. Fold the end of the bag several times and secure with paper clips. Keep the bag away from oven elements. Bake at 425°F/220°C for 45–50 minutes, or until the apples are tender and the topping golden.

TO SERVE:

Serve warm with a scoop of vanilla ice cream.

JAMES, CAITLIN AND OWEN'S BIRTHDAY CAKE

Serves 8–10

Kids especially love the mystery and fun of making cookies and cakes. Jamie and Elaine Pitblado encourage this in their children, even if their kitchen looks as if a hurricane just flew by. The children love to take over to whip up the best chocolate cake you could ever wish for on your birthday. Caitlin takes charge and her brothers follow the head baker's directions! Our daughter-in-law is on their "very special" list for their now-famous birthday cake; we all give a big cheer as Suzie blows out the candles, makes a wish and cuts the cake. Don't forget to add a scoop of vanilla ice cream! Jamie and Elaine say, "We've sure cut down on the cleaning up in the kitchen by starting with a cake-mix base! You would never guess it's not from scratch."

1	package Duncan Hines Devils Food Cake Mix	
1	package Jell-O chocolate instant pudding mix	
8 oz	chocolate chips	200 mL
1 cup	sour cream	250 mL
1 cup	water	250 mL
½ cup	vegetable oil	125 mL
3	large eggs	3

METHOD:

Preheat the oven to 350°F/180°C. With an electric mixer, blend the ingredients in order, adding the wet ingredients slowly and the eggs one at a time, until just blended, about 2 minutes. Don't overbeat. Pour into a greased and floured 10-in / 25-cm, flat-bottom Bundt pan. Bake for 60–65 minutes, or until the cake tester comes out clean and the middle of the cake springs back when pressed with a finger. Cool. If made a day ahead, wrap and seal well. Sprinkle with icing sugar before serving.

Desserts

ICE CREAM WITH ESPRESSO AND FRANGELICO

Serves 2

This ice cream extravaganza is your dessert, coffee and liqueur rolled into one! Jill Krop named it "the adults' milkshake" as I was making it on our "Saturday Chefs" Global TV series. Our friends Charmaine Crooks and husband Anders Thorsen ordered this ice cream delight on our visit to a popular rooftop bistro in Del Mare, California. It was the perfect choice for the balmy evening as we sat watching the local scene.

4 scoops vanilla ice cream, or combined with a scoop of chocolate or coffee ice cream
Frangelico or Bailey's liqueur
Strong espresso coffee, freshly brewed
Shaved Callebaut or Godiva chocolate
Italian biscotti

METHOD:

Just before serving, brew the coffee. Place 2 scoops of ice cream in each heatproof goblet or bowl. Drizzle over a little of the liqueur. Pour over a little coffee. Sprinkle with the shaved chocolate and serve immediately with a biscotti or other Italian cookie on the side. Magnifico!

CHOCOLATE
ALMOND VELVET

Makes about 18, using large muffin baking cups

What a treat to pull out of the freezer! This ice cream dessert is so easy to make and so popular that everyone wants the recipe. These are truly like velvet, very smooth and creamy. Great for summertime and Christmas entertaining. They are also a hit at children's parties.

10 oz	can chocolate syrup	300 mL
1 pt	whipping cream	475 mL
10 oz	can Eagle Brand sweetened condensed milk	300mL
½ tsp	vanilla	2.5 mL
1 cup	toasted almonds or almond roca candies, finely chopped	250 mL

METHOD:

In a bowl, combine the chocolate syrup, cream, condensed milk and vanilla. Chill in the refrigerator for about 1 hour. Whip until fluffy and the mixture forms soft peaks; don't overwhip, or it will separate. Fold in ½ cup /125 mL of the chopped nuts or almond roca candy. Put paper cups in muffin tins and fill each just to the top of the cups. Top each with the remaining nuts or almond roca and freeze, uncovered, until firm. Store in airtight freezer container until needed.

Serve with fresh strawberries, if desired. Serve immediately from the freezer, as these melt quickly!

DIANE'S SECRETS:

For children's parties or for those who love malt balls, use Buddies Malt Balls or Maltese balls, coarsely chopped, instead of the nuts or almond roca — sensational!

MANGO-LIME CHAMPAGNE ICE

Serves 6–8

On our visit to Singapore Doug and I came across a dessert stand that featured shaved ice as a base, with numerous chopped fruits with fruit syrup and purée toppings. The customers had a choice of more than 20 combinations and the staff prepared everything in front of you. It was wild!

The story goes that when the owner was buying this company he thought the name of the business was "Dessert Mouse." He had a mouse logo designed and his staff and all his signs sported his new emblem, a little mouse after the name. But when he went to sign the final papers he discovered that the name was actually "Dessert House"! Since he had already gone ahead with all his mouse logos, he decided to leave the name as "Dessert Mouse." It does get your attention!

I came home and played around with his ice concept, adding a bit more sophistication with champagne in the sorbet base. It's totally refreshing!

¾ cup	**fine berry sugar**	175 mL
⅜ cup	**water**	90 mL
1	**ripe mango, peeled, pureed**	1
	(about 1 cup/250 mL)	
3 tbsp	**lime juice**	45 mL
25 oz	**bottle champagne or**	750 mL
	sparkling white wine	

TOPPING:

1	**ripe mango, peeled, pureed**	1
	(about 1 cup /250 mL)	
1	**ripe mango, peeled, finely chopped**	1
20 oz	**can lychee fruit, drained,**	500 g
	cut in half	

METHOD:

Several days ahead of serving, place the sugar and water in a small saucepan over high heat. Bring to boil, stirring until the sugar dissolves. Place the sugar syrup in a large bowl with the mango purée, lime juice and champagne. Stir to blend. Pour into a plastic container (11 ½ × 8 × 2 in / 28 × 20 × 5 cm). Seal well and place in the freezer.

Stir with a whisk or fork every 20–25 minutes for the first few hours of freezing, to give the ice a smooth consistency. Serve when frozen.

TO SERVE:

Spoon into martini glasses or sherbet dishes. Drizzle a little of the mango purée over the ice. Top with a little chopped mango and the lychee fruit. Serve immediately.

BANANA ICE WITH BERRY PURÉE

Serves 4–6

Low-cal ice cream? It can't be, it's so creamy and rich! Believe it! I call it my "energy revitalizer." Whenever you have too many ripe bananas, pop them into the freezer and you have the beginnings of an instant soft ice cream to satisfy any craving.

ripe frozen bananas
vanilla or fruit yogurt
raspberry or strawberry purée
fresh berries

METHOD:

A day or two ahead of serving, or weeks ahead, peel 4 or 5 ripe bananas or more, freeze in sealed plastic containers (bananas should be fully ripe, but not dark). Allow four to five hours for them to freeze.

Just before serving, cut the frozen bananas into chunks and zap in food processor with about 3 tbsp/45 mL vanilla or fruit yogurt and whirl just until thickened and creamy; it should be like soft ice cream. Spoon about 2 tbsp/30 mL of raspberry purée into a wine goblet or sherbet dish, place a few spoonfuls of banana ice on top and garnish with fresh raspberries or sliced fresh strawberries.

RASPBERRY OR
STRAWBERRY PURÉE:

Purée 2 cups/500 mL of fresh or frozen unsweetened raspberries or strawberries, then strain in a fine-mesh strainer. This can be made days ahead and refrigerated, or frozen and thawed overnight in the refrigerator.

ITALIAN ICE CREAM CAKE
WITH RASPBERRY SAUCE

Serves 12

This has been one of my most popular desserts from the time it was first printed in the original *Chef on the Run*. I have served it for many family birthdays, with Italian menus, as Christmas dinner instead of the traditional plum puddings, and for many barbecue finales! Another ideal make-ahead dessert.

¾ cup	white sugar	175 mL	
⅓ cup	water	80 mL	
3	egg yolks	3	
	dash salt		
1 cup	crumbled almond macaroon cookies or amaretti cookies	250 mL	
8–10	ladyfingers	8–10	
4 tbsp	Grand Marnier, white rum or sherry	60 mL	
1 pt	whipping cream	475 mL	
2 tsp	vanilla	10 mL	
½ tsp	almond extract	2.5 mL	

METHOD:

Line a 6–8-in/15–20 cm mould or soufflé dish with foil. In a small saucepan, combine the sugar and water and bring to a boil over medium heat, stirring until sugar is dissolved. Boil gently without stirring to 230°F/110°C on a candy thermometer, or until a little of the sugar mixture spins a thread when dropped from a spoon.

In a medium bowl, with mixer at medium speed, beat yolks and salt until light. Gradually beat in the hot syrup in a thin stream, continuing to beat until mixture begins to cool, about 2 minutes. Stir in the macaroons and refrigerate for about 10 minutes. Sprinkle ladyfingers with the liquor.

Combine cream with flavourings and beat until stiff. Fold whipped cream into macaroon mixture. Turn half the mixture into the prepared mould. Make a layer with ladyfingers and pour in the remaining mixture. Freeze, well sealed (it will keep for weeks).

RASPBERRY SAUCE:

2	**packages frozen raspberries, thawed**	2
2 tbsp	**cornstarch**	30 mL
½ cup	**red currant jelly**	125 mL

GARNISH:

additional whipped cream

chocolate curls

METHOD:

Drain raspberries, reserving liquid; there should be enough liquid to make 2 cups/500 mL. In a small saucepan, blend the liquid with cornstarch and bring to boil, stirring constantly. Continue to boil for about 5 minutes, or until thickened. Stir in the jelly until melted. Remove from heat, add raspberries. Cool, cover and refrigerate. This can be made a day or two ahead of serving.

TO SERVE:

Unmould and serve on a rimmed cake plate; spoon raspberry sauce around the base and decorate the top with additional whipped cream and chocolate curls.

AZTEC ICE CREAM
WITH LIME SAUCE

Serves 4–6

Glenys Morgan, one of Vancouver's most sought-after and respected chefs for cooking classes, came up with this unusual and enticing Aztec Ice Cream when we both conducted a Southwest-theme class. It was a triumph! Serve it after the Tex-Mex dinners **Mexican Torta** (pg. 186), or **Cal-Mex Chicken Fiesta** (pg. 184).

1 qt	**vanilla ice cream**	1 L
3 tbsp	**dark rum**	45 mL
1 tsp	**cinnamon**	5 mL
½ tsp	**dried red pepper flakes**	2.5 mL
	slices of lime (for garnish)	

METHOD:

In a medium-size bowl, soften the ice cream slightly. Fold in the rum, cinnamon and red pepper flakes. Freeze in a sealed container until ready to serve. Can make a day or two ahead of serving.

LIME SAUCE:

	zest of 4 large limes	
1 cup	water	250 mL
1 cup	sugar	250 mL
1 ½ tbsp	vanilla (Mexican if available)	7.5 mL

METHOD:

In a saucepan, heat the water and sugar until the sugar is dissolved. Add the zest of limes and slowly bring to boil. Turn it down and simmer until the rinds are translucent, about 10 minutes. Remove from heat and cool to room temperature. Add the vanilla, refrigerate. Can be made a day or two ahead of serving.

TO SERVE:

Put a scoop of the ice cream into a wine goblet. Drizzle the lime sauce over. Garnish with a thin slice of lime.

LIZ'S HEAVENLY LEMON MOUSSE

Serves 6

I had so much fun doing the food shoots with Liz and Jack Bryan, publishers of the first four books in my *Chef on the Run* series. Former publishers and owners of *Western Living Magazine*, Liz was my editor and Jack the official food photographer. They both happen to be excellent cooks, as well, and Liz's lemon mousse dessert was included in *More Chef on the Run*. This dessert is a light and refreshing finale to any meal. The mousse can be made the day ahead and refrigerated, or frozen a couple of weeks ahead, as it freezes beautifully. Just bring it out of the freezer a few hours before serving, and refrigerate. The first pick of sweet summer raspberries would be a perfect match for the tartness of the lemons.

1 tbsp	**gelatin**	15 mL
¼ cup	**cold water**	60 mL
5	**large eggs, separated**	5
	zest of 1 lemon, grated finely	
¾ cup	**lemon juice**	175 mL
1 ¼ cup	**white sugar**	310 mL
1 cup	**whipping cream**	250 mL

METHOD:

Sprinkle gelatin over cold water to soften. Mix egg yolks with lemon juice and rind and ¾ cup of the sugar, cook in a double boiler or a thick-bottomed pan on low heat, stirring constantly until it is thick enough to coat a spoon, about 8–10 minutes.

Remove from heat and stir in the softened gelatin. Chill for 30–40 minutes. Beat egg whites until stiff, gradually add the rest of the sugar and continue to beat. Whip the cream until stiff. Fold cream gently into whites, then fold both into the lemon custard. Pour into individual soufflé dishes or goblets and chill or freeze.

FRENCH FRUIT CLAFOUTIS

Serves 6–8

A clafoutis is simply a custard-like dessert with fruit added and baked. The classic French clafoutis is usually made with sweet dark cherries, but I like it as well with mixed fruits. It's one of those comfort desserts that goes well with a hearty country-style dinner such as **Basil Roast Chicken with Garlic Sauce** (pg. 177).

4 cups	mixed fresh fruit, any combination of peaches, pears, apricots, nectarines, raspberries, cherries, plums, or use one fruit only	1 L
4	large eggs	4
⅔ cup	white sugar	160 mL
⅓ cup	white flour	80 mL
1½ cups	milk	375 mL
	OR	
¾ cup	each milk and half-and-half	175 mL
2 tsp	vanilla	10 mL
	pinch of salt	

METHOD:

In a food processor, blend the eggs, sugar, flour, milk (or blend of milk and half-and-half), vanilla and salt until smooth. Let sit for about 15 minutes while you prepare the fruit.

For skinned fruits, peel, core and cut into thin slices. For plums and cherries, remove the pit or seed and cut into thin slices.

Butter one medium glass or gratin casserole and sprinkle with sugar to coat. Spread the fruit in the baking dish. Pour the batter evenly over the fruit, covering all evenly. Bake in a 400°F/200°C oven for 35–45 minutes, or until the batter puffs up and is golden and a knife inserted in the middle comes out clean. Keep checking from the 35-minute mark on; the timing depends on what type of fruit you are using. The clafoutis should have a custard-like consistency.

CRÈME FRAICHE:

1 cup	**sour cream**	250 mL
1 cup	**whipping cream**	250 mL

METHOD:

In a bowl, gently whisk the sour cream and cream until just blended. Cover and leave at room temperature for at least 24 hours. Stir and refrigerate; it will thicken as it chills. Will keep for about 1 week.

TO SERVE:

Clafoutis is filling, so give small portions. Serve warm with whipped cream, vanilla ice cream or crème fraiche.

DIANE'S SECRETS:

You can make the clafoutis ahead of time and reheat in a 350°F/180°C oven for about 20 minutes until warmed, but it is best made just before serving. The ingredients can be prepared early in the day and refrigerated until ready to bake, but keep the fruit and the egg mixture separate; assemble just before popping into the oven.

CHAMPAGNE ZABAGLIONE BERRY GRATIN

Serves 4, recipe can be doubled

If you really want to impress your guests with an elegant, sensual finale, this is the dessert for you! One of Vancouver's restaurant chefs saw me making this dish on my Global Television "Saturday Chefs" spot and he decided to do it for his customers that evening. In his haste, he left the berry gratin under the broiler too long, and when he went to check it, it was charcoal on top! So remember, don't leave to do something else: keep your eyes on the gratin under the broiler.

	raspberry or strawberry sorbet	
1 cup	**each of sliced**	250 mL
	strawberries, raspberries and blueberries	

CHAMPAGNE ZABAGLIONE:

4	**large egg yolks**	4
½ cup	**fine berry sugar**	125 mL
½ cup	**champagne or other sparkling wine**	125 mL

DIANE'S SECRETS:

You can make the zabaglione early on the day of serving. Place in a bowl, cover and refrigerate. To serve, whisk the zabaglione slightly before dividing it equally on top of the fruit. Broil the fruit as directed or serve chilled over berries.

METHOD:

In a medium bowl, toss the berries together on the morning of serving. Divide evenly among 4 shallow gratin dishes. Cover with plastic wrap and set aside until ready to serve. If you wish, toss 3 tbsp /45 mL Grand Marnier or other orange liqueur with the berries.

Just before serving, heat a little water in a large stainless steel mixing bowl; water should be hot, but not boiling. In a smaller stainless steel bowl, whisk the egg yolks and sugar until they are pale and foamy. Stir in the champagne, place the bowl inside the large bowl with the hot water in it. Beat constantly with a wire whisk until the custard has doubled in bulk and begins to thicken, 5–8 minutes. Remove from the hot water and drizzle the zabaglione evenly over the top of the fruit in each of the gratin dishes. Place the gratin dishes under the broiler until golden, watching all the time! Put on serving plates, place a small scoop of the sorbet in the middle of each gratin dish and serve immediately.

MANGO and RASPBERRY CRISP

Serves 8

One of my favourite fruits is mango, as you can tell from the number of recipes in which I have included this fabulous fruit! What a dynamite duo — mango and raspberries baked with a crisp hazelnut topping and served warm. As our son Rand says, "Yummmmmie!"

FRUIT:

6	mangoes, peeled, sliced into 1-in / 2.5-cm pieces	6
2 cups	fresh raspberries	500 mL
¼ cup	lemon juice	60 mL
6 tbsp	sugar	90 mL
2 tbsp	flour	30 mL

METHOD:

In a bowl, combine the mangoes, lemon juice, sugar and flour and mix well. Set aside. Add the rasperries to the reserved mangoes and spoon into a shallow casserole or 8 small, shallow ramekins.

CRISP:

1 ⅓ cups	hazelnuts or almonds, finely ground	325 mL
	pinch of salt	
1 ½ cups	flour	375 mL
⅔ cups	sugar	160 mL
¾ cups	butter	175 mL

METHOD:

In a medium bowl, blend the hazelnuts, salt, flour and sugar. Cut in the butter with 2 knives or a pastry cutter until the mixture is crumbly; continue working in the butter until completely incorporated and there are no dry crumbs. Squeeze mixture together to create clumps from pea size to ½ in /1 cm.

TO SERVE:

Sprinkle the nut-and-flour mixture on top of the casserole, or on top of each ramekin, allowing some of the fruit to show through. Bake at 375°F/190°C until the top is golden brown and the fruit juices are thick and bubbling, 35–40 minutes. Remove from oven, place on a wire rack until slightly warm. Serve with a scoop of vanilla ice cream or mango or raspberry sherbet just before serving.

MOM'S **APPLE BREAD PUDDING** WITH **MAPLE SAUCE**

The ultimate in bread puddings is one that our mother whipped up for our family while we were growing up in Moncton, New Brunswick. Like many family recipes, this is one that her mother and grandmother served. Sometimes different fruit is added, depending on the season. Most bread puddings tend to be dry and boring, but not this one! Whenever I serve this Maritime version, it brings raves. It is one of the all-time top "comfort desserts." Use day-old French or sourdough bread, croissants or brioches.

6 cups	**bread, crusts removed**	1.5 L
	and cut into 1/2-in /.5-cm cubes	
1 tbsp	**vanilla**	15 mL
1/4 cup	**pure maple syrup**	60 mL
	large Granny Smith or Newton apples,	
	peeled, cut into small cubes,	
	tossed with 2 tbsp / 30 mL sugar	
5 cups	**milk**	1.25 L
1/2 cup	**raisins or raspberries**	125 mL
	(fresh or frozen)	
3	**large eggs**	3
1 cup	**white sugar**	250 mL
1/2 tsp	**fresh nutmeg,**	2.5 mL
	grated or ground	
	whipped cream	

MAPLE SAUCE:

1	**large egg**	1
6 tbsp	**butter, melted**	90 mL
1 cup	**icing sugar**	250 mL
1 tsp	**vanilla**	5 mL
1/4 cup	**pure maple syrup**	60 mL

METHOD:

One night or several hours ahead, combine the bread with the vanilla, maple syrup, apples, milk and raisins until mixed. Cover and refrigerate.

When ready to bake, preheat the oven to 350°F/180°C. In a bowl, whisk the eggs, sugar and nutmeg well. Pour over the bread mixture and mix gently. Pour into a greased 8 × 11-in/20 × 27.5-cm glass lasagna-type baking dish. Bake for about 1 hour, or until the dessert has puffed up and is golden, with a custard-like texture. Remove from the oven, pour maple sauce (below) evenly over the top. Serve warm, topped with whipped cream sweetened with a little maple syrup, or vanilla ice cream.

While the pudding is baking, in a small saucepan whisk the egg and add the melted butter gradually. Add the icing sugar, vanilla and maple syrup. Simmer on low heat, stirring constantly, until the sauce has thickened slightly. Can be made a day ahead if you wish; bring to room temperature and spread over the bread pudding when ready.

BERRIES in CHAMPAGNE JELLY

Serves 4

This is definitely an adults' party Jell-O! Try this whimsical light dessert at your next summer dinner party to perhaps bring back memories of your childhood, but with a touch of sophistication.

3 ½ cups	**mixed berries**	875 mL
	(strawberries, blueberries	
	and raspberries)	
½ cup	**water**	125 mL
¼ cup	**berry sugar**	60 mL
1 tbsp	**gelatin**	15 mL
6.5 oz	**bottle well-chilled**	200 mL
	Champagne or sparkling white wine	
	raspberry or strawberry	
	sorbet (optional)	

METHOD:

A day ahead, divide the mixed berries evenly among four martini glasses or sherbet dishes. Set aside.

In a small saucepan, combine the water and sugar, stir over low heat until the sugar is dissolved. Remove from heat, sprinkle the gelatin in and mix with a small whisk until the gelatin is dissolved. Slowly add to the chilled champagne or sparkling wine and mix just to blend.

Top the four berry-filled glasses or sherbet dishes evenly with the wine mixture and refrigerate for at least 4 hours to set.

TO SERVE:

Top with a small scoop of berry sorbet.

MANGO PANNA COTTA

Serves 6

This is one of the most sensuous desserts you can eat! On one of our trips to Sydney, Australia, all the hottest restaurants were serving panna cotta, which they described as "sweet cream" — and so it is. This presentation is a total "mango" experience, but you can use your imagination in choosing other purées, or add coffee for a change of flavours. It's so easy and quick to make, but could be made a day ahead.

PURÉE:

1	ripe mango, peeled, chopped (about 1 cup/250 mL)	
2 tsp	lime juice	10 mL

CREAM MIXTURE:

1	envelope unflavoured gelatin	1
1 tbsp	boiling water	15 mL
2 cups	whipping cream	500 mL
1/3 cup	whole milk	80 mL
1/2 cup	white sugar	125 mL
1/2 tsp	vanilla	2.5 mL

METHOD:

Combine in a food processor until smooth. Set aside.

Put boiling water in a small heatproof dish. Sprinkle gelatin in and whirl well with a fork to remove any lumps. Set aside for a few minutes, or until the gelatin dissolves and the mixture is clear.

In a medium saucepan, combine the whipping cream, whole milk, sugar and vanilla. Simmer over low heat, stirring occasionally for about 10 minutes. DO NOT BOIL.

Add a little of the hot cream mixture to the gelatin mixture and stir to blend. Then add to the rest of the warm cream mixture and blend until the gelatin has dissolved. Pour in the reserved mango purée and blend well.

JUST THE FACTS — MANGOES

Mangoes continue to ripen after they are picked, so you can choose fruit that is still slightly green and firm. Mangoes originated in India and are believed to strengthen the heart and improve brain function! They are an excellent source of vitamins A and C, calcium and iron, and are easily digested.

Pour the mixture evenly into 6 (½-cup /125-mL) custard ramekin dishes. Cover with plastic wrap and refrigerate for at least 6 hours, or overnight.

TO SERVE:

Quickly dip the moulds into a bowl of warm water, then loosen the panna cotta with a knife if necessary before carefully tipping out onto a dessert plate.

GARNISH:

1	mango, peeled, sliced into thin strips (like spaghettini)	
1	mango, peeled, chopped, puréed	
1	kiwi, peeled, thinly sliced	
	mango sorbet	

Garnish each plate with a small cluster of thin strips of mango, drizzle the plate with a little purée, add a slice of kiwi and a small scoop of mango sorbet.

STRAWBERRY OR RASPBERRY PANNA COTTA: Substitute 1 cup /250 mL of strawberry or raspberry purée for the mango and decorate your plates with a little of the berry purée, a few berries and a berry sorbet.

COFFEE PANNA COTTA: Eliminate the mango or fruit purée. Add ¼ cup / 60 mL finely ground coffee or espresso to the whipping cream, whole milk, sugar and vanilla mixture. Simmer as directed above, for about 10 minutes. DO NOT BOIL. Then pour the coffee cream liquid through a fine strainer to filter out the coffee grounds. Follow the directions up to tipping out onto dessert plate. Garnish with a few chocolate coffee beans and a chocolate biscotti, if desired.

RASPBERRY AND
WHITE CHOCOLATE TART

Serves 6–8

This luscious tart, filled with a creamy Italian mascarpone cheese-white chocolate filling marbled with raspberry coulis, rates a 10! This summertime dessert is divine.

SWEET PASTRY CRUST:

1 cup	**flour**	250 mL
¼ cup	**sugar**	60 mL
⅓ cup	**chilled butter**	80 mL
1	**egg, slightly beaten**	1

METHOD:

Combine flour and sugar, cut in the butter until mixture resembles coarse meal. Stir in the egg, mixing well. Wrap and chill for about 30 minutes, then roll out to line a 9-in/22.5-cm flan pan with removable sides. Press pastry well into bottom and up the sides, prick with fork. Line with foil (shiny side down) and weight with a few dried beans. Chill for about 30 minutes.

Preheat the oven to 375°F/190°C. Bake the pastry for 15 minutes, then remove the foil and beans, drop the oven temperature to 350°F/190°C, and bake for another 15–20 minutes, or until the pastry is golden and crisp. Cool completely, then remove from the tin. Set aside. Can be made a day ahead, wrapped with plastic wrap and left at room temperature.

RASPBERRY COULIS:

1 pt	**fresh raspberries**	475 mL
2 tbsp	**honey**	30 mL

Reserve a few raspberries for the top of the tart. Put the rest in a small pan with the honey. Bring to a boil and simmer for 3–5 minutes to reduce the sauce a little. Remove from the pan, press through a fine sieve and cool. Set aside.

MASCARPONE-WHITE CHOCOLATE FILLING:

4 oz	white chocolate, chopped	100 g
1 cup	mascarpone cheese	250 mL
	(from specialty cheese delis)	
2 tbsp	white rum	30 mL
⅔ cup	cream	160 mL

TOPPING:

	reserved raspberries	
2 oz	white chocolate curls	50 g

METHOD:

Put the 4 oz /100 g white chocolate, mascarpone and rum into a bowl set over simmering water, stir until it melts into a smooth sauce. Leave to cool to room temperature. Whip the cream until it holds its peaks, then fold into the chocolate mixture. Roughly stir in half the cool raspberry coulis to get a marbled effect. Spoon into the pastry case and chill for about 30 minutes so that filling sets softly.

TO SERVE:

Scatter the reserved raspberries and curls of white chocolate on top. Pass the remaining coulis.

JUST THE FACTS — MASCARPONE

Mascarpone is a rich, slightly tart, thick cream that originated in Italy in the 16th century. It's one of the key ingredients in the popular Italian tiramisu dessert.

For a quick and decadent topping for fresh fruit, gently fold 1 cup /250 mL of room-temperature mascarpone with ½ cup /125 mL whipped cream and 2 tbsp /30 mL orange liqueur, or ½ tsp /2.5 mL vanilla.

ACKNOWLEDGEMENTS

I was inspired by my family, friends and cooking students to write my first cookbook, *Chef on the Run*, to share my passion for cooking. *Chef on the Run* is now celebrating its 20th birthday and *Chef on the Run: Simply the Best* is a birthday present to all those who have eaten their way through all those many family recipes, and still come back for more!

My husband, Doug, has encouraged me from the very first experimental recipe I had him taste. He has been my star taster, mentor and fun coach, patiently going into markets, gourmet shops and kitchen boutiques around the world, then loading our suitcases with my newly found food treasures and utensils for our journey home.

Our children Jennifer, and Rand, have been my joy and my daughter-in-law, Suzie, and son-in-law, Vincent, have made my family complete. I love testing my newest recipes on them all at our Sunday dinners!

My wonderful parents, Rand and the late Lou Matheson, and my brothers Joel and David, and sisters-in-law, Ruth and Dianne, have always been there for me. I must acknowledge our roots in the Maritimes, where I was taught how to produce total comfort food in Mom's kitchen.

As well, I thank: Maurice and Pat Clement who have been the backbone of our Clement Clan and continue to be our role models.

Charmaine Crooks and husband Anders Thorsen, who have shared our Olympic experiences and our family times.

Sharon Woyat, Don and Marcelle McLean and their family for their encouragement.

Also, special thanks to:

Arnold Gosewich, my book agent, who keeps me on my toes and whose guidance and expertise have been immensely appreciated.

Liz and Jack Bryan, founders of *Western Living Magazine*, my first publishers and mentors in learning about the delicious career of cookbook writing!

The Raincoast Books team: Allan MacDougall, Mark Stanton (now retired) and Kevin Williams, who had faith to distribute the four "Chef On The Run" series and later published *Diane Clement at the Tomato* and *Zest For Life* (in 2001, *Zest For Life* won a bronze Canadian Culture cookbook award from Cuisine Canada), Michelle Benjamin, for her support and input; Derek Fairbridge and Ingrid Paulson, for their fresh ideas and enthusiasm for *Chef On The Run: Simply the Best*; and Tessa Vanderkop, dynamic Raincoast publicist, who has always been "on the run" promoting my books.

Barbara Watts, Devine Elden, Jeto Hundal and Helen Nachtigal, my longtime friends and my gold medal team for all my cooking classes, book launches and special receptions.

The "Gourmet 8" gals, who still whip up gourmet fare for our luncheons after 37 years!

Cooking schools: Cindy Evetts Tools and Technique, Caren McSherry's Valagao's, and many more over the years!

Television hosts Jennifer Mather and Jill Krop, who taught me how to "play to the camera" for the "Saturday Morning Chefs" series on BCTV, now Global.

CTV's Vicki Gabereau for her wit and charm that kept her audience and me laughing the whole time as we cooked up a storm on her popular show, *Vicki Gabereau Live*.

Special kudos to:

John Sherlock, the brilliant food photographer who makes every picture tantalize all our taste buds. The great bonus of producing the 16 shoots in three days for my books is that we do not rely on artificial touch-ups — what you see is exactly how your own dishes should look when you prepare them in your own kitchen.

John's talented assistant, Alastair Bird, the Raincoast team and friends all looked forward to sampling all the dishes I prepared for each day's shoot!

Lightheart and Company Gourmet Gifts and Tableware in Vancouver — owner Sherri McEwan, Gabriela Berlinghof in corporate sales and the knowledgeable staff — let me loose to choose the fabulous white dishes to complement the food for the photo shoots. I had a field day. They have everything you could ever imagine for entertaining and for that special gift.

I also thank Barbara-Jo MacIntosh, owner of Books to Cooks cookbook store in Vancouver, and resident store chef, Adrienne O'Callaghan, for their assistance and for providing the shooting location for my "Saturday Chefs" TV spots on Global.

Finally, a big thank you to Les Dames d'Escoffier, Vancouver chapter for their support in all my food ventures, and for the fun times.

INDEX